Published by Wandel Guides, June 2014	**Hard Copy Edition**
Martin Smit, info@pinkdot.nl	**Graphic Design and Maps**
978-1492811893	**ISBN-13**
1492811890	**ISBN-10**
www.hiking-in-jordan.com	**Website**
hikinginjordan@gmail.com	**Email**
"Near Wadi Rum's Seven Pillars of Wisdom", by Grant & Maassen	**Cover Image**
CreateSpace, an Amazon.com Company	**Printed by**

Grant & Maassen
Hiking in Jordan

With trails in and around Petra,
Wadi Rum, Wadi Mujib,
Wadi Araba, Rahma
and the Dead Sea

Contents

Jeep Safari

Mushroom Rock

Preface and Acknowledgments

Chris Grant

This Hiking in Jordan Guide would not have been possible without the support of a large number of friends who tirelessly spent numerous hours exploring hiking areas with the authors. Our thanks go out to Dr. Tom Carson, Razan Abd El Haque, Andrea Conrad, Jane Sedgely, Rob Strachan, Feras Ajlouni, Janet Beasley, Tim and Xochitl Bartlett, Janet Katz, Prof. Bill Kosar, Marieke Lettink, Janita Sluurman and Frank de Weerd for joining us while we documented trails in Jordan. We especially acknowledge the contribution of Jackson Grant, who flew in from Australia to assist with the production of the hiking videos and the design of trails. Mike and Terri Scadron and Jane Mahoney flew in from the United States and Martin and Esther Smit from the Netherlands to test our itineraries.

A Big Thanks to Everyone

A special thanks goes out to Shama Sallam and Ahmad Eid Ahliwat who, through dedication and enthusiasm, ensured that we fully appreciated the beauty of Wadi Araba and the wonderful Bedouin communities living in and near Rahma. In a similar vein, we thank Salem Zalabih of "Mohammad Mutlak Camp" and his family and friends for welcoming us frequently to his community in Wadi Rum. We also would like to acknowledge Susie Shinaco of the Bait Ali Lodge, for sharing her knowledge of Wadi Rum that led us to the French Fortress and the magnificent dunes in Disi.

We are also grateful to the managers of the Wadi Rum Protected Area, Park Manager Nasser Zawideh,

H.E. Commissioner Mohanad Hararah and H.E. Commissioner Sharhabeel Madi of ASEZA for their support and enthusiasm promoting sustainable tourism in Jordan.

Gregory Maassen

We are grateful to Jan Anfouka and Reem Saadeh for their friendship and support saving us from difficulties while we explored the country. They were always one phone call away to translate and provide interpretation services when the authors were in trouble. We would also like to recognize the work of Jacky Bedrossian, the author of "Say it in Arabic", and her lovely daughter Lilly for their help providing translations. Our special thanks go out to Emad Qasaymeh of the Aqaba Astronomy Association and his family for building an amazing observatory in Wadi Rum, which brought us frequently to the desert watching the stars at night.

We are also grateful to our graphic designer Martin Smit for his outstanding work creating the lay out of this book and producing the hiking maps. We are also grateful to Mike and Terri Scadron, JoAnn Bordeaux, Judy Macaluso, Andrea Conrad, Fran Paver, Dan Pelletier, Samantha Winter, Paulette Fried, Shadi Tanash, Andrew Bennett, Prof. Bill Kosar, Jane Mahoney, Chris Lehmann and Janet Katz, for proofreading and critiquing drafts of the guidebook.

Our special thanks go out to Ms. Claire Brennan for her outstanding support by proofreading large sections of the draft and to Gregory Pellechi for his valuable contribution as senior editor of the guidebook.

Thank you for your support *and being a hiker in Jordan. Please do not hesitate to contact us if you have any questions. We welcome any feedback you may have.*

We would also like to thank you, the users of this book. By purchasing this book, you not only make it possible for us to develop more hiking guides, but more importantly, by visiting Jordan, exploring its beauty and interacting with its communities, you substantially contribute to the sustainable development of the country.

Chris Grant & Gregory Maassen
hikinginjordan@gmail.com

Introduction

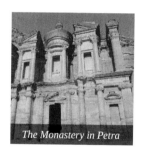

The Monastery in Petra

Jordan is a beautiful and hospitable country that should be on every traveler's itinerary. While it is mostly known for superb cultural sites such as Petra and Jerash, plush resorts on the Dead Sea and package Bedouin experiences at Wadi Rum, there is much more than this to Jordan.

Jordan's Diversity

Its people are diverse, its history and culture rich and there are ancient castles, rock inscriptions, tombs and temples. Above all else, there are massive landscapes to explore and unlimited hiking to enjoy. This is a country where, if you want, you can escape the crowds and explore the wilds very easily and safely, yet retreat to a comfortable hotel whenever you choose. Your most enduring memories of Jordan will be of the decency and friendliness of the people, the desert silence, starry skies and vast and awe-inspiring landscapes.

Jordan's History

Officially called the Hashemite Kingdom of Jordan, it has a population of over 6 million people from a variety of tribal and ethnic groups. The country arose from the post-World War I division of the Middle East by Great Britain and France after the collapse of the Ottoman Empire. It was under British mandate until May 25, 1946, when it was recognized by the United Nations as an independent sovereign kingdom. It is a constitutional monarchy ruled by His Majesty King Abdullah II with an elected parliament. In a region beset with strife, Jordan is a remarkably stable and safe country.

When to Go Although Jordan is a small country, you will find wide variations in climate due mostly to altitudinal differences. In mid-winter, the Dead Sea, at 423 meters (1,388 ft) below sea level, can be balmy; Aqaba at sea level will be pleasant while Wadi Rum, Petra and Amman at some 800 meters (2,624 ft.) to 1,000 meters (3,280 ft.) above sea level will be chilly and may have snow. In contrast, summer in Jordan is excruciatingly hot with temperatures exceeding 40 °C (100 °F) along the Dead Sea and in the south. During this time it is mostly too hot to hike. Outside of summer, with planning you can do great hiking at any time, though spring is best. The countryside will be at its greenest and the temperature will be pleasant everywhere.

Online Resources

A variety of resources and planning tools that accompany the Hiking Guide are available at the Hiking in Jordan website (www.hiking-in-jordan.com).

Trail Videos: For each of the 32 main trails there is a High Definition video providing an overview of the trail. You can watch the videos on our website and YouTube Channel.

Trail Animations: Using NASA World Wind technology, we have produced an animated "3D" overview for each main trail. These are great for researching an area prior to a hike.

Trail Photos: You will find over 1,000 trail photos on the website licensed under Creative Commons (CC BY-SA). Please contact us if you would like to use the images under a different license.

Siqs and Wadis

A Siq is a narrow canyon. Wadi is the Arabic term for valley.

Google Earth™ Maps: You can explore the hiking trails using the Google Earth™ KML files. These files are useful for virtually exploring an area before heading out. The Google Earth™ KML files are available on the website to registered owners of the Hiking Guide.

GPS E-trails: Each trail is designed with the independent traveler in mind. Even without a GPS device, you can enjoy many of the trails in this Hiking Guide using the maps provided. We nevertheless recommend that you bring a GPS device and have it loaded with Hiking in Jordan E-trails. They are available on the website to registered owners of the Hiking Guide in GPS eXchange Format - GPX, Google Earth™ and Garmin™ formats[1].

To access the E-trails and other resources available to owners of this book, you will need to register on our website: *www.hiking-in-jordan.com*

During the registration process, you will be asked for a registration key.

Please enter the following key: *amazon145e321*

Hiking Tutorials: These are video tutorials on preparing for your hiking trip in Jordan. Topics range from what to bring on hiking trips to flash flood awareness. The hiking tutorials are available on our website and YouTube Channel.

The Hiking in Jordan Music Collection: Each trail video and animation is accompanied by a soundtrack. There are over 40 soundtracks in the collection that you can download from the website.

The "Off the Record" Video Collection: You may want to check out this special collection of goofy videos. While we were working on the Hiking Guide, we ran into unexpected and funny situations. The Off the Record video collection is available on our website and YouTube Channel.

Please Note

The GPS files on the Hiking in Jordan website are provided exclusively to owners of the Hiking Guide.

---

1 Google and the Google Logo are registered trademarks of Google Inc. Garmin is a registered trademark of Garmin Corporation. These firms are not associated with the Hiking in Jordan Guide.

The Trails

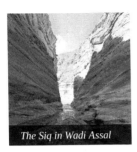
The Siq in Wadi Assal

Very few people hike independently in Jordan and there are hardly any established or signposted trails. For this reason, bringing a GPS device and utilizing the E-trails we provide will save you time planning your holiday.

Hiking Regions in Jordan

The trails in this Hiking Guide have been grouped into four regions:

- *The North:* This covers the area north of Amman including Pella and Ajloun.
- *The Dead Sea:* Most trails near the Dead Sea are located in valleys (wadis), including the famous Wadi Mujib.
- *Petra and Central Jordan:* This area covers the central part of Jordan including Petra, Dana, Mukawir and Feynan.
- *Wadi Rum and Southern Jordan:* The trails in this area are located in the deserts of Wadi Rum and Wadi Araba south of the Dead Sea.

Trail Classification

Easy: These routes are appropriate for novice hikers. They are usually easy to follow, being along a wadi, track or road, but do not expect any trail signs. Grades are gentle and relatively few obstacles will be encountered.

Moderate: These routes are appropriate for intermediate through advanced hikers. Terrain is steeper and more obstacles may be encountered. Do not expect any trail signs or obvious trail paths you can follow.

Advanced: These routes are recommended for experienced hikers. Terrain may be steep and routes are not obvious. You should be able to navigate and must be self-reliant.

Trails	Duration	Level	4X4 Car needed?	Distance	
	[HOURS]			[MI]	[KM]
Northern Jordan					
01 Ajloun Castle Circuit	1.5	Easy	No	2.5	4.0
02 Ajloun Castle Trail	3.5	Easy	No	5.0	8.0
03 Pella Mountain Trail	4	Moderate	No	5.2	8.4
04 Wadi Zubia Forest Walk	4	Easy	No	5.4	8.7
Petra and Central Jordan					
05 Dana Feynan Trail	6	Moderate	No	8.7	14.0
06 Little Petra Canyon Trail	4	Moderate	No	4.3	6.9
07 Mukawir Mini Circuit	1.5	Easy	No	0.7	1.1
08 Petra High Place of Sacrifice Trail	8	Moderate	No	10.9	17.5
09 Petra Monastery Trail	7	Moderate	No	9.7	15.6
10 Rummana Mountain Trail	2	Easy	No	2.2	3.5
11 Wadi Bin Hammad Tropical Rain Forest Trail	1.5	Easy	No	2.5	4.0
12 Wadi Ghuweir Trail to Feynan	8	Advanced	No	9.3	15.0
The Dead Sea					
13 Wadi Al Karak Waterfalls	5.5	Easy	No	7.8	12.6
14 Wadi Assal	5	Moderate	No	7.0	11.3
15 Wadi Attun Hot Springs Trail	2.5	Moderate	No	1.4	2.3
16 Wadi Himara Palm Trees and Waterfall Trail	2	Moderate	No	2.1	3.4
17 Wadi Himara Panorama Trail	2	Moderate	No	1.7	2.7
18 Wadi Mujib Malaqi Trail	4.5	Moderate	No	4.3	6.9

TRAILS		DURATION	LEVEL	4X4 CAR NEEDED?	DISTANCE	
		[HOURS]			[MI]	[KM]
19	Wadi Mujib Siq Trail	2.5	Easy	No	1.1	1.8
20	Wadi Mukheiris Formation Trail	3.5	Moderate	No	3.6	5.8
21	Wadi Numeira Siq Trail	5	Easy	No	5.6	9.0
22	Wadi Weida'a	2	Easy	No	1.8	2.9
Wadi Rum and Southern Jordan						
23	Abu Barqa Dam Lookout	2.5	Moderate	No	2.4	3.9
24	Adami Trail - Jordan's Tallest Mountain	3	Moderate	Yes	1.8	2.9
25	Bedouin Camp Circuit	2.5	Easy	Yes	3.8	6.1
26	Burial Mound and Oryx Trail	6	Advanced	No	9.0	14.5
27	French Fortress Trail	3.5	Moderate	No[1]	6.9	11.1
28	Ibex Canyon Lookout	5	Advanced	No	5.3	8.5
29	Lawrence of Arabia Spring	2.5	Moderate	No	3.0	4.8
30	Nabatean Temple Trail	3.5	Moderate	No	3.4	5.5
31	Rahma Bedouin Camel Trail	4.5	Advanced	Yes[2]	6.3	10.1
32	Seven Pillars of Wisdom	4	Moderate	No	6.3	10.1

1 Unless the access road is covered with sand.

2 Unless you add 1.6 km (1 mile) one way to the trail hiking from the Dead Sea Highway.

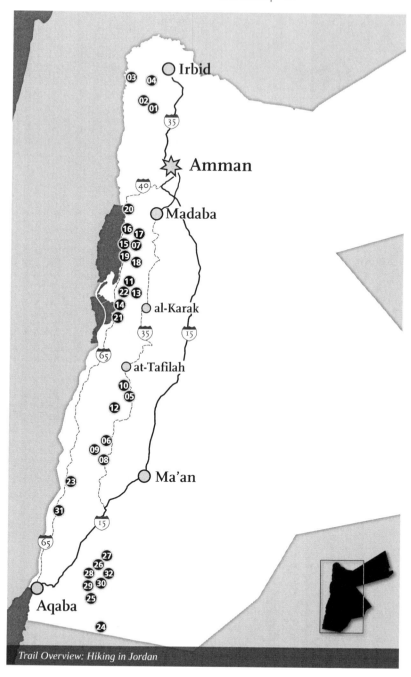

Trail Overview: Hiking in Jordan

On Top of Jebel Adami, Jordan's Tallest Mountain

Sample Travel Itinerary

From Aqaba to Amman/Madaba
7 Days

The Seven Pillars of Wisdom

Arrival in Aqaba   Day 1

While in Aqaba you may want to visit the beach and shop for souvenirs, sort out a rental car, and get bottled water and snacks for the trails.

Wadi Rum   Day 2

You can make an early start with the Seven Pillars of Wisdom Trail *(» page 251)* near the Wadi Rum visitors' center. Then have lunch and take a couple of hours to explore the Lawrence of Arabia Spring Trail *(» page 230)* near Wadi Rum village. You can take a camel ride to a Bedouin camp, or a Jeep tour in the afternoon and watch the beautiful sunset while drinking Bedouin sage tea. If you have time, you can walk the Bedouin Camp Circuit *(» page 200)* in the afternoon.

For the more adventurous, drive to the base of Jebel Um Adami and camp before hiking to the summit of Jordan's tallest mountain.

Wadi Rum to Petra   Day 3

Hike the Adami Trail in the early morning *(» page 194)* or any other trail in Wadi Rum if you have the energy. On the way out, don't forget to also consider the French Fortress Trail *(» page 214)*. You can drive to Petra (1.5 hours) from Wadi Rum, check into a hotel and enjoy the sunset (we recommend that you look for a hotel with a rooftop area).

Day 4 *Petra*
We recommend that you head into Petra early to beat the crowds and ensure you have a full day of hiking. The Petra High Place of Sacrifice Trail *(» page 76)* will take you around most of Petra. You can always backtrack down the trail from the Monastery if you run out of steam. Relax in your hotel after a day in Petra and enjoy local food and hospitality in Wadi Musa.

Day 5 *Visit Karak or Wadi Bin Hammad and Madaba*
In the morning, we suggest that you hike the Little Petra Canyon Trail *(» page 59)*. Continue north to Dana for the Rummana Mountain Trail *(» page 100)* or to Karak for a visit to the castle and/or the Wadi Bin Hammad Tropical Rain Forest Trail *(» page 105)*. Take time to absorb the views at Mujib Canyon, then continue on to Madaba to stay for the night.

Day 6 *A Full Day of Exploration Near Madaba*
A nice day trip option is the Wadi Mujib Malaqi Trail near the Dead Sea *(» page 155)*, but remember that this is a tour that you have to book with the RSCN in advance. If you can't get on a tour, we suggest the Wadi Mujib Siq Trail instead *(» page 162)*. On the way back to Madaba, you may have time for either the Wadi Attun Hot Springs *(» page 138)* or the Wadi Himara trails *(» pages 143 and 149)*. Nearer to Madaba is the Mukawir Mini Circuit for great views of the Dead Sea *(» page 69)*.

Tip
Drink plenty of water while you travel to your hiking site. This way, you will have to consume less water while hiking.

Day 7 *Arrival in Amman/Stay in Madaba*
Unless you have a pressing desire to go to Amman, you may want to stay in Madaba a second night as it is closer to the airport. In Madaba, you can check out the mosaics, the nearby Mount Nebo, buy souvenirs or explore any remaining hikes. In Amman, you can explore the restaurants, shopping malls, the Roman theater and the citadel.

With a couple of extra days available, after Petra, you can explore the Wadi Ghuweir Trail to Feynan *(» page 112)* and camp or stay in the Feynan Lodge. On the second day you can walk on to Dana village via the Dana Feynan Trail *(» page 52)*.

Day Trips from Aqaba		Road Distance - One Way	Road Distance - One Way	Car Travel Time - One Way	Main Roads
		[mi]	[km]	[hours]	[route]
Petra and Central Jordan[1]					
06	Little Petra Canyon Trail	84.5	136	3	15, 35
08	Petra High Place of Sacrifice Trail	79.5	128	3	15, 35
09	Petra Monastery Trail	79.5	128	3	15, 35
The Dead Sea					
13	Wadi Al Karak Waterfalls	143	230	3	65
14	Wadi Assal	131	211	2.5	65
18	Wadi Mujib Malaqi Trail[2]	139	224	3.5	65
19	Wadi Mujib Siq Trail	139	224	3.5	65
21	Wadi Numeira Siq Trail	127	204	2.5	65
22	Wadi Weida'a	139	223	3	65
Wadi Rum and Southern Jordan					
23	Abu Barqa Dam Lookout	49	78.6	1.5	65
24	Adami Trail - Jordan's Tallest Mountain[3]	55.9	89.9	4.5	15
25	Bedouin Camp Circuit	50.1	80.6	3	15
26	Burial Mound and Oryx Trail	39	62.7	1.5	15
27	French Fortress Trail	40.6	65.3	1.5	15
28	Ibex Canyon Lookout	39	62.7	1.5	15
29	Lawrence of Arabia Spring	43.4	69.8	1.5	15
30	Nabatean Temple Trail	43.4	69.8	1.5	15

DAY TRIPS FROM AQABA	ROAD DISTANCE - ONE WAY	ROAD DISTANCE - ONE WAY	CAR TRAVEL TIME - ONE WAY	MAIN ROADS
	[MI]	[KM]	[HOURS]	[ROUTE]
31 Rahma Bedouin Camel Trail	36.9	58.4	1.5	65
32 Seven Pillars of Wisdom	39	62.7	1.5	15

Route 15 = The Desert Highway
Route 35 = The King's Highway
Route 65 = The Dead Sea Highway

You can use the Google Earth™ KML files available at *www.hiking-in-jordan.com* to explore driving directions to the hiking areas.

1 The earlier you leave Aqaba, the better. We recommend that you stay overnight in Wadi Musa the day before you explore Petra.

2 Please check the RSCN website for times when the organized group leaves in the morning. The group normally leaves at 8 AM.

3 It is 20 km (12.5 miles) and at least 1.5 hours by 4x4 car to reach the trail from Wadi Rum village so it is best to stay overnight in Wadi Rum the day before.

Day Trips from Amman[1]	Road Distance - One Way [mi]	Road Distance - One Way [km]	Car Travel Time - One Way [hours]	Main Roads [route]
Northern Jordan				
01 Ajloun Castle Circuit	42.6	68.6	2	35
02 Ajloun Castle Trail	42.6	68.6	2	35
04 Wadi Zubia Forest Walk	44.6	71.7	3	35
Petra and Central Jordan				
07 Mukawir Mini Circuit	42.4	68.2	2	35
11 Wadi Bin Hammad Tropical Rain Forest Trail	92.6	149	3	35
The Dead Sea				
15 Wadi Attun Hot Springs Trail	43.7	70.4	2	40, 65
16 Wadi Himara Palm Trees and Waterfall Trail	36.4	58.6	2	40, 65
17 Wadi Himara Panorama Trail	40.5	65.2	2	40, 65
18 Wadi Mujib Malaqi Trail[2]	49.5	79.6	2.5	40, 65
19 Wadi Mujib Siq Trail	49.5	79.6	2.5	40, 65
20 Wadi Mukheiris Formation Trail	32.6	52.4	1.5	40, 65

Route 35 = The King's Highway
Route 65 = The Dead Sea Highway

1   Distances and travel times are approximate and measured from the 7th Circle in Amman.

2   Please check the RSCN website for times when the organized group leaves in the morning. The group normally leaves at 8 AM.

Hiking Safety

Safety on the Trail

Travel Advisories   Before traveling, we recommend that you check with your embassy or ministry of foreign affairs for the latest travel advisories for Jordan. Many countries have a "Smart Traveler Enrollment Program", where you register your trip intentions and receive important safety and security announcements.

Jordan is considered a very safe country to travel. Visitors are made welcome and assistance is always forthcoming when requested. The danger of violence towards tourists is low. The dangers you are most likely to encounter are related to traffic accidents.

Share Hiking Details   When going to remote places, it may be some time before your absence is noticed if you have not left a plan of your intentions. It is important to notify someone reliable of your hiking intentions, including where you will start and finish, how you are traveling, members and nationalities of your group, vehicle details, phone numbers of group members and when the alarm should be raised. Leaving behind a note in the car explaining what you are doing is often a good idea. You can download travel notes that you can leave in the car from our website.

Communication   You may want to carry at least one mobile phone. Having SIM cards of the main mobile phone carriers improves your chances of getting phone reception while you are in remote areas.

About 70 percent of Jordan's rain falls between November and March, mainly in January and February. There is a real danger of flash floods during the rainy season when you hike in valleys (wadis), especially in narrow, rocky valleys near the Dead Sea such as Wadi Assal, Wadi Mujib and Wadi Mukheiris. Wadis surrounded by solid rock formations can experience very rapid run-off when it rains.

Flash Flood Awareness

Avoid hiking in the narrow wadis if there is any chance of rain upstream. Warning signs while in the wadi include a stream rising quickly with muddy water and a roaring sound upstream. We strongly recommend that you head immediately for higher ground whenever you see indications of a flash flood. Because of flash floods and general high water levels, the RSCN closes the Wadi Mujib reserve between November and March.

Tip

Watch the video on flash flood awareness on our website (www.hiking-in-jordan.com) and the Hiking in Jordan YouTube Channel.

When hiking in remote areas, we recommend that you:

Safety Summary

- **Prepare.** Hike at home, keep fit and know your limitations. Carefully choose and be familiar with your equipment and learn first aid. Before a hike, investigate the terrain, conditions and local weather.
- **Leave your plans with someone.** It is always a good idea that you tell someone where you are going, when you'll return and leave details of your vehicle, phone numbers and group size and composition.
- **Stay together.** When you start as a group, hike as a group and end as a group. Pace your hike to the slowest person.
- **Turn back when it is wise to do so.** Fatigue and difficult terrain may slow you down. Don't blindly persevere; stop and reassess your plans.
- **Know how to handle an emergency.** Even if you are headed out for just an hour, an injury, severe weather or a wrong turn can be life threatening. Don't assume you will be rescued in Jordan; know how to rescue yourself.

Water Management

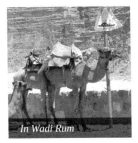

In Wadi Rum

It is vital to carry plenty of drinking water while hiking in Jordan. Dehydration is a big danger in Jordan. There are a variety of methods to carry water but we recommend that you use a CamelBak™ or similar system[1]. You can sip on water while you're walking, without the need to stop and open your backpack to find a bottle of water.

While drinking during the hike is very important, it is equally imperative that you hydrate yourself before you start. Have a big drink of water while you are on your way to the trail. Try to consume at least one liter of water in the hour before the hike.

Sun Protection

The sun in Jordan can be incredibly intense especially in the summer. You will suffer sorely if you do not protect yourself from the sun.

You need a good hat, and a light cotton scarf is also a good idea. Take lightweight trousers and a long-sleeve shirt. Take plenty of sunscreen and use it on all exposed parts of your body. Keep it on hand in a side pocket of your pack. Sunglasses are a good investment because the desert landscape produces a lot of glare.

Emergency Contacts

Emergency	911	(toll-free)
Ambulance	199	(toll-free)
Tourist Police	196	(toll-free)
	06 569 0384	(land line)
	077 672 8446	(Orange mobile)
	079 712 3080	(Zain mobile)
Jordanian Police	191	(toll-free)
	0795 513 729	(land line)
Traffic Police	190	(toll-free)
Highway Patrol	194	(toll-free)

Emergency Equipment

We recommend that you bring a first aid kit with a collection of plasters of various sizes, as well as triangular, regular and compression bandages and antiseptic. Despite the high temperatures in summer, it can also be cold in Jordan, especially at night. If

1 CamelBak is a registered trademark of CamelBak, Inc.

there is an emergency, keeping warm is important. Space blankets are inexpensive, very light and highly effective keeping the body warmth in. They are also a high visibility item that assists rescuers in finding you.

If you need rescue or are separated from other hikers, attracting attention is vital. We recommend that you carry:

Attracting Attention

- **Some high visibility items** (e.g., bright clothing or space blanket).
- **A mirror** – on a sunny day this can attract attention from many kilometers away.
- **A whistle**.
- **A flashlight** and spare batteries. A headlamp is best.
- **Matches or lighter** to make a fire to attract attention through light or smoke and to keep warm.

We recommend that you upload the E-trails from our website onto your GPS. Don't forget spare batteries for the GPS. For added security, you can use a lanyard to secure the GPS to your belt to prevent it being lost.

Know Where You Are: GPS Devices and Maps

If you have a sprained ankle, you will appreciate having hiking poles. Even if you don't use them, lightweight collapsible poles in your pack will be no burden. They are handy on broken and slippery ground, or if you find yourself out in the dark, and are good to take pressure off your knees on descents.

Hiking Poles

Regular snacks will keep your energy levels up, which is especially important if you are out longer than expected. Jordanian date bread is a good energy food and can be found locally in bakeries and supermarkets. Nuts and dates can be found in most shops and service stations. Falafel sandwiches are everywhere. You can get fruit in supermarkets and seasonal fruit is often sold by the road.

Stay Happy: Comfort on the Trail

Hiking in Jordan Checklist

HIKING IN JORDAN CHECKLIST	
Drink plenty during breakfast, prior to, and during the hike	Hiking poles
Bring plenty of water on the trail in a CamelBak™ or similar system	Sturdy hiking boots with good ankle support
Protect yourself from the sun with clothing, a hat, scarf and sunscreen	Cell phone with essential telephone numbers and local sim card
First Aid kit	A GPS with our E-trails pre-loaded
Space blanket	Spare batteries for GPS
Flashlight and headlamp	A copy of the Hiking in Jordan Guide
Spare batteries	Food
Whistle	Extra socks and shoes (in the car)
Lighter and/or matches	Toilet paper and hand disinfectant
Mirror/compass with mirror	Sample notes you can leave in the car near the trail
Pocket knife	Pen and paper

Tip

Check out our recommendations for hiking gear on www.hiking-in-jordan.com. Each purchase you make through our website supports this and our other hiking projects under development.

You will be surprised how easily the few essential items fit into a daypack.

Snakes, Spiders and Scorpions

You are unlikely to see any dangerous animals while hiking in Jordan, but you should be aware Jordan has some venomous creatures. As with all wildlife, do not disturb it and only observe it from a safe distance. Wearing boots with ankle support and trousers is an excellent way of protecting yourself from these little creatures.

Readers' Feedback

Do you have ideas or suggestions for trails in Jordan? Noticed something we can improve upon? We welcome your feedback. You can reach us at *hikinginjordan@gmail.com* and through the contact form on our website.

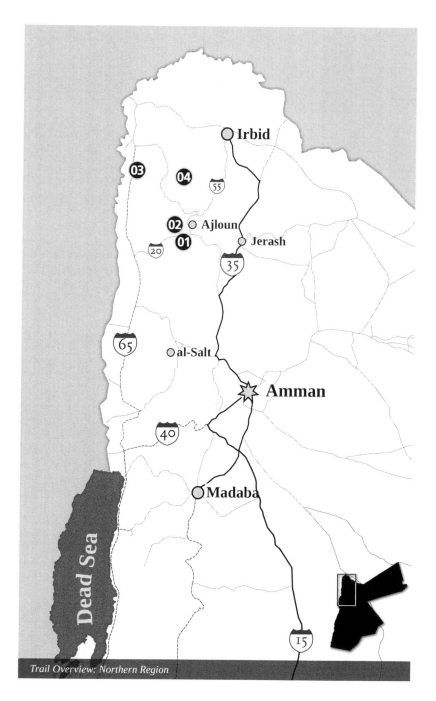

Trail Overview: Northern Region

Wadi Zubia Forest

Region
Northern Jordan

01 Ajloun Castle Circuit
02 Ajloun Castle Trail
03 Pella Mountain Trail
04 Wadi Zubia Forest Walk

Ajloun Castle Circuit

Introduction

Located north-west of Amman, the Ajloun Castle Circuit is a short walk around the Ajloun Castle (Qal'at Ajloun or Qal'at Ar-Rabad) that takes you through pleasant rolling limestone hills with terraced slopes and olive groves. You will obtain fine views of the Ajloun Castle from all angles.

This is a shorter version of the Ajloun Castle Trail *(» page 33)*. The walk is solely on paved roads circumnavigating the castle and is a very easy 4 km (2.5

View of the Castle from the Valley

miles) hike that gets you away from the crowds. A guide or GPS device is not required. You can combine the walk with a visit to Jerash for a full day trip from Amman.

Trail Description   From the parking lot near the visitors' center, walk straight up the road towards the castle entrance for 200 m (650 ft.). Before the castle entrance, take the paved road to the right. Follow the paved and winding road for about 1.5 km (0.9 miles) until you reach the first T-junction overlooking the valley. Make a left turn and stay on the main road. Do not take the road on your right into the valley.

Follow the road with the castle on the hill top ahead of you (on the left), while the valley is on your right. After 1.4 km (0.9 miles), you come to another T-junction. Turn left and follow the road in the direction of the castle for 600 m (0.4 miles). Turn left to the parking lot where you can visit the castle for more views of the area.

- The castle originally had four towers when it was erected by one of Saladin's generals in 1184 AD. They have since been toppled by earthquakes.
- In 1215 AD, the castle was expanded under the Mamelukes' rule and is a good example of Arab and Islamic military architecture in Jordan.
- It was initially built to control the iron mines in the area, to protect the three main routes leading to the Jordan Valley and trading routes between Jordan and Syria, and was part of a defensive chain against the Crusaders.
- It is believed that a message could be transmitted from Damascus to Cairo in less than twelve hours using pigeons and fire/smoke through the chain of castles and signposts of which Ajloun Castle was an integral part.

About the Castle

From Amman **Getting There**

The Ajloun (or Ajlun) Castle is near the town of Ajloun and can easily be reached by car. The castle is not far from the Ajloun Nature Reserve, Jerash and Wadi Zubia *(» page 44)*. Drive from Amman in the direction of Jerash and Irbid on Route 35. Make a left turn onto Route 20 and follow directions to Ajloun. Make a right turn onto Route 55. In the center of Ajloun, make a left turn at the traffic lights and drive uphill towards the Ajloun Castle. Park your car near the visitors' center.

Be aware that the gate to the car park near the visitors' center may close after 4 PM. To be on the safe side, you can park your car on the road. Tickets to the castle can be bought at the visitors' center.

			Video Notes
0:12	-	The Ajloun Castle (Qal'at Ajloun or Qal'at Ar-Rabad).	
0:41	-	The road circumnavigating the castle.	
1:30	-	The castle seen from the main road in Ajloun leading to the visitors' center.	

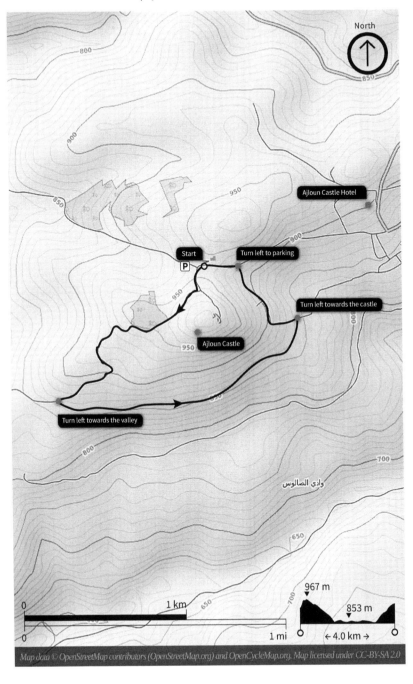

North

Ajloun Castle Hotel

Start
P
Turn left to parking

Turn left towards the castle

Ajloun Castle

Turn left towards the valley

وادي الصالوص

0

1 km

0

1 mi

967 m
853 m
← 4.0 km →

GPS FILE	01 AJLOUN CASTLE CIRCUIT
Duration:	1.5 hours
Level:	Easy
Starting Point Coordinates:	N32 19.677 E35 43.637
Starting Point:	Ajloun Castle parking lot.
Is a Four Wheel Drive Car Required?	A 4x4 car is not required. You can park a normal car at the visitors' center.
Distance:	4 km (2.5 miles)
Highest Point:	967 m (3,173 ft.)
Lowest Point:	853 m (2,798 ft.)
Difference in Elevation:	114 m (375 ft.)
Trail Type:	Circular Trail
Is a GPS Device Required?	No
The Nearest Point with Amenities:	The visitors' center has toilets and you are near the town of Ajloun with hotels and restaurants.

About the Area

The area around the castle contains remnants of Mediterranean vegetation that was once widespread in this part of Jordan. Apart from the ubiquitous olive groves, you will find mostly Evergreen Oak. The nearby Ajloun Forest Reserve is said to still have wild boar, Stone Marten, Golden Jackal, Red Fox, Striped Hyena, Persian Squirrel, Indian Crested Porcupine and wolves. Roe Deer were reintroduced there after becoming locally extinct.

02

Ajloun Castle Trail

Introduction This is a longer version of the Ajloun Castle Circuit *(» page 28)*. This easy hike is mainly on gravel roads and can be combined with a visit to Jerash if you plan for a full day of traveling from Amman. The trail is 8 km (5 miles). A guide or GPS device is not required.

Trail Description The trail starts at the parking lot near the visitors' center of Ajloun Castle. From the parking lot, turn right and walk towards the valley downhill on a paved road with stone walls on both sides.

After 650 m (0.4 miles), you will see a dead end road to the right. Ignore this and all other roads that go to the right while you are in the valley. Follow the main road for another 2.3 km (1.4 miles) as it descends into the valley with terraced hillsides. The road levels out and you come to an intersection with another dead end road to the right. Continue to follow the main road.

You will pass stone walls on both sides of the main road. Soon thereafter, the road curves to the left and starts to climb. The gravel road turns into an asphalt road which you should follow while you keep ascending for 2.1 km (1.3 miles).

You pass some buildings on the right and after 100 m (0.2 miles) you come to a Y-junction. Follow the road to the right and stay left to follow the main road with the valley on your right. Do not take the road on your right into the valley.

GPS FILE	02-1 AJLOUN CASTLE TRAIL	02-2 AJLOUN CASTLE TRAIL
Duration:	3.5 hours	3 hours
Level:	Easy	Easy
Starting Point Coordinates:	N32 19.677 E35 43.637	N32 19.677 E35 43.637
Starting Point:	Ajloun Castle parking lot.	Ajloun Castle parking lot.
Is a Four Wheel Drive Car Required?	A 4x4 car is not required. You can park a normal car at the visitors' center.	A 4x4 car is not required. You can park a normal car at the visitors' center.
Distance:	8 km (5 miles)	6.9 km (4.3 miles)
Highest Point:	949 m (3,112 ft.)	977 m (3,205 ft.)
Lowest Point:	641 m (2,104 ft.)	641 m (2,104 ft.)
Difference in Elevation:	308 m (1,008 ft.)	336 m (1,101 ft.)
Trail Type:	Circular Trail	Circular Trail
Is a GPS Device Required?	No	No
The Nearest Point with Amenities:	The visitors' center has toilets and you are near the town of Ajloun with hotels and restaurants.	The visitors' center has toilets and you are near the town of Ajloun with hotels and restaurants.

Follow the road with the castle on the hill top ahead of you (on the left), while the valley is on your right. After 1.4 km (0.9 miles), you will come to a T-junction. Turn left and follow the road in the direction of the castle for 600 m (0.4 miles). Turn left to reach the car park where you can visit the castle for more views of the area.

Extended - Alternative E-trail Version

We have included a slightly shorter version of the trail in the E-trail collection. The Ajloun Castle Trail - Route 2, is approximately 30 minutes and 1.1 km (0.7 miles) shorter. Instead of following the road to the right after you pass buildings and when you come to a Y-junction, you turn left and walk straight towards the castle following the road uphill. Please see the GPS files for more information.

Notes, Getting There

See Ajloun Castle Circuit (» page 28).

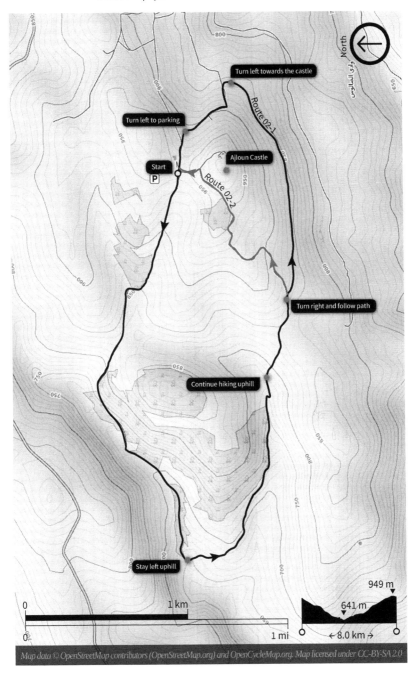

Video Notes

0:15 - We walked from our hotel in Ajloun to the parking lot at the castle near the beginning of the trail.

0:19 - The Ajloun Castle (Qal'at Ajloun or Qal'at Ar-Rabad).

0:26 - The road on the right side of the parking lot leads downhill into the valley. You can recognize the beginning of the trail by the stone walls on both sides of the road.

1:04 - The road circumnavigating the castle.

1:18 - Halfway along the trail, you walk uphill after you leave the valley.

1:42 - The castle is on top of the hill on your left ahead of you, near the end of the trail.

The Castle in Ajloun

Northern Jordan

03 Pella Mountain Trail

Introduction Not far from the Syrian border and near the Jordan Valley, the ancient site of Pella is located on the slope of Jebel Sartaba.

The hike is a healthy walk around the oak-dotted limestone hills of Pella near the archaeological site of Tabaqat Fahl, the name of the nearby village. With sweeping views of the Jordan Valley, there are Byzantine and Roman ruins as well as evidence of Bronze and Iron Age settlements spread throughout the area.

It is believed the Romans developed Pella as an economic center in the second century of the Christian era. Early settlements in Pella date back over 8,000 years.

The trail does not require a guide or GPS device. You will be walking uphill on some sections of the trail with a total difference of 379 m (1,241 ft.) in elevation during the hike, but you will be rewarded with magnificent views of the area.

Trail Description From the asphalt road, walk through the little entrance gate to the archaeological site. When you enter Pella, you immediately will see the complex with the columns. This prominent structure is a basilica from the Byzantine period.

After you have wandered through the site, follow the track towards the trees below leaving the basilica behind. Find your way through the old fence near the water pump station a few hundred meters (900 ft.) from the basilica. Follow the track to the left up the hill in the direction of Jebel Sartaba, the small mountain on your left above the wadi. Follow the trail uphill to the right for a minute and turn to the left through a stony and relatively barren area with some scattered oaks and hike up the hillside. Do not go into or cross the wadi on the left.

Continue hiking towards the mountain in an easterly direction with the wadi on your left and Pella behind you. After 1 km (0.6 miles) you have reached the first hill. Walk around to the top of the hill for magnificent views of the Jordan Valley.

After having conquered the first hill, take the trail that leads up to the mountain on the left (keep Pella behind you). Do not take the track on the right that descends near the hillside. You walk up the mountain on a gravel service road to the Hellenic Ruins on top of the mountain.

After checking out the Hellenic ruins, continue walking to the nearby top of Jebel Sartaba to the east and descend into the valley with farm land until you reach a dirt road (1.1 km/0.7 miles) and go left. Stay left at the next junction and follow the asphalt road until you cross a wadi after 1.9 km (1.2 miles). You come to a T-junction with the main road leading back to Pella. Just before the T-Junction, walk to the top of the hill on your left and head back on the plateau to Pella. You will have a large wadi on your left and the main road to Pella in the distance on your right. Continue walking on the top of the hill for 1.9 km (1.2 miles) until you reach a fence enclosing the archaeological site near the Pella Guesthouse, which provides luncheons and a nice view of Pella.

From Irbid   Getting There

If you come to the Jordan Valley from Irbid on Route 10, you will need to make a left turn when you meet Route 65. Set your odometer at this intersection; the turn-off to Pella is 18.4 km (11.5 miles) south of here. You will pass the turn-off to the Sheikh Hussein

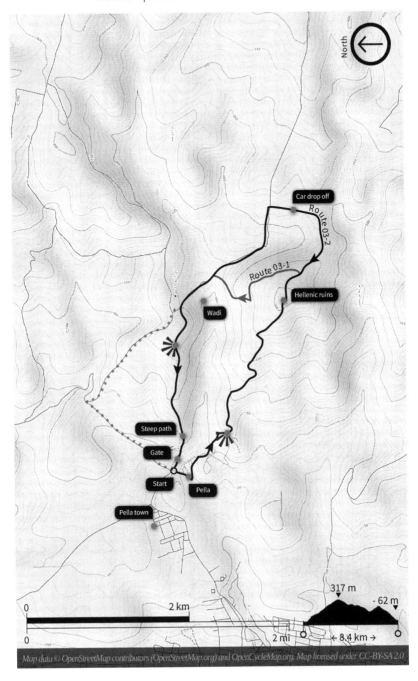

North

Car drop off

Route 03-2

Route 03-1

Hellenic ruins

Wadi

Steep path

Gate

Start

Pella

Pella town

0 — 2 km

0 — 2 mi

317 m

- 62 m

← 8.4 km →

Map data © OpenStreetMap contributors (OpenStreetMap.org) and OpenCycleMap.org. Map licensed under CC-BY-SA 2.0.

GPS FILE	03 PELLA MOUNTAIN TRAIL
Duration:	4 hours
Level:	Moderate
Starting Point Coordinates:	N32 27.046 E35 36.938
Starting Point:	At the entrance to Pella.
Is a Four Wheel Drive Car Required?	A 4x4 car is not required. You can park near the entrance to Pella.
Distance:	8.4 km (5.2 miles)
Highest Point:	317 m (1,039 ft.)
Lowest Point:	-62 m (-202 ft.)
Difference in Elevation:	379 m (1,241 ft.)
Trail Type:	Circular Trail
Is a GPS Device Required?	A GPS device is not required, but recommended.
The Nearest Point with Amenities:	The Pella Guest House is adjacent to the archaeological site. You will find hotels in Ajloun.

Bridge border crossing on the right, also known as the Jordan Valley Crossing. From this intersection, drive 5.8 km (3.6 miles) south. You will see the turn-off to Pella (Tabaqat Fahl) on your left. Drive up the road and follow signs to the site which is just a few hundred meters east of the little village.

From Amman or Ajloun

Pella is in the vicinity of the Jordan Valley 130 km (81 miles) north of Amman. If you drive on Route 65 somewhere north of the Dead Sea, whether you come from Amman or Ajloun, you will need to drive north towards the border with Syria. Continue driving north until you see the turn-off to Pella (Tabaqat Fahl) on your right. If you come to the turn-off to the Sheikh Hussein Bridge, you have gone too far. Turn around and drive back 5.8 km (3.6 miles). You will

At Pella

see the turn-off to Pella (Tabaqat Fahl). Drive up the road and follow signs to the site which is just a few hundred meters east of the little village.

About Pella

- The ruins were "re-discovered" in 1818 by the Hon. Captain Charles Leonard Irby and Captain James Mangles of the British Royal Navy.
- The archaeological site was purchased by the Jordanian government in the 1970s to preserve the area.
- The small settlement of Tabaqat Fahl was located on top of the main mound in Pella near the entrance until it was relocated to preserve the archaeological site.
- The site is actively researched and excavated by the Near Eastern Archaeology Foundation in conjunction with the Pella Excavation Project of the University of Sydney.
- Archaeologists have been working on the site for over thirty years.

Other Notes

- The best time to hike is in spring when an abundance of flowers blossom on the hillsides.
- Although there are no signposts outside the ancient site, it is easy to follow well established tracks to return to Pella.

Video Notes

- 0:41 - The little gate to the Pella archaeological site near the asphalt road.
- 0:50 - The basilica.
- 1:00 - Do not go into the wadi or cross the wadi below on the left. Stay on the path and walk up the hill on the right side of the wadi.
- 1:07 - The gravel service road leading up to Jebel Sartaba.
- 1:34 - The Hellenic ruins near the top of Jebel Sartaba.

Extended Alternative E-trail Versions We have included in the E-trail collection two additional trails. The Pella Mountain Ridge Trail is a slightly shorter but more demanding hike leaving established paths. You need to descend towards the wadi before hiking on the hillside that leads back to Pella.

You can also download an E-trail that leads to a car drop-off point in case you like to hike a shorter distance and someone can drop you off. The file is named "03-2 Pella Mountain Trail-Car Drop Off."

GPS FILE	03-1 PELLA MOUNTAIN RIDGE TRAIL	03-2 PELLA MOUNTAIN TRAIL - CAR DROP OFF
Duration:	3.5 hours	2.5 hours
Level:	Moderate	Easy
Starting Point Coordinates:	N32 27.046 E35 36.938	N32 26.337 E35 38.524
Starting Point:	At the entrance to Pella.	At car drop-off point.
Is a Four Wheel Drive Car Required?	A 4x4 car is not required. You can park near the entrance to Pella.	A 4x4 car is not required. You can park near the drop-off point.
Distance:	7.1 km (4.4 miles)	4.7 km (2.9 miles)
Highest Point:	316 m (1,038 ft.)	317 m (1,039 ft.)
Lowest Point:	-61 m (-200 ft.)	-62 m (-202 ft.)
Difference in Elevation:	377 m (1,238 ft.)	379 m (1,241 ft.)
Trail Type:	Circular Trail	Linear Trail (one way)
Is a GPS Device Required?	A GPS device is not required, but recommended.	A GPS device is not required, but recommended.
The Nearest Point with Amenities:	The Pella Guest House is adjacent to the archaeological site. You will find hotels in Ajloun.	The Pella Guest House is adjacent to the archaeological site. You will find hotels in Ajloun.

Wadi Zubia Forest Walk

This trail is located in Wadi Ain Zubia (Zubiya or Zoubia) in the Northern Jordanian Highlands. This area offers great hiking opportunities. The trail takes you through Roman ruins, dense forests and the small village of Zubia with views of the valley below. Other than in the wadi, you walk on established paths. This area has been settled for a long time, with the first settlements in Zubia village dating back to the Byzantine period.

Introduction

Don't be surprised if you see local treasure hunters with shovels and pickaxes in the area as the rumor must be still out there that gold is to be found under the Roman ruins.

The wadi is part of the Zubia Forest which has some of the world's southernmost surviving pine and evergreen forests. The wadi is located north of the RSCN managed Ajloun Forest Reserve and is a favorite location of locals who enjoy the coolness of the forests in the north. Bird watchers might like to watch out here for the Palestine Sunbird, the Upcher's Orphan and Sardinian Warblers.

From the parking area, the trail starts at the Roman ruins, although do not expect to see a restored historic site. There is not much to see other than foundations and building blocks. From the ruins, descend for a minute or two into a field leading into the wadi. After 300 m (0.2 miles), the open field narrows with trees on both sides. A path should become visible here.

Trail Description

GPS FILE	04 WADI ZUBIA FOREST WALK
Duration:	4 hours
Level:	Easy
Starting Point Coordinates:	N32 25.546 E35 45.932
Starting Point:	Entrance to the wadi.
Is a Four Wheel Drive Car Required?	A 4x4 car is not required. You can park a normal car in the parking area near the wadi.
Distance:	8.7 km (5.4 miles)
Highest Point:	921 m (3,022 ft.)
Lowest Point:	635 m (2,082 ft.)
Difference in Elevation:	286 m (940 ft.)
Trail Type:	Circular Trail
Is a GPS Device Required?	A GPS device is not required, but recommended.
The Nearest Point with Amenities:	In the town of Zubia you may find some shops. There are hotels in Ajloun and the RSCN lodge in the Ajloun Forest Reserve.

Follow the trail into dense forest for about 220 m (0.14 miles) until you see the creek. Follow it down into the valley for 1.6 km (1 mile) to an interesting rock formation located in the creek. The rocks make for a great picnic spot. Moving on, after 800 m (0.5 miles) you enter an open area with the wadi widening ahead of you. You will see a gravel service road.

Walk along the service road to the left for nice views, then turn back and walk uphill on this road for 2.7 km (1.7 miles) until you reach an asphalt road. Turn right and follow the road immediately to the right towards the town of Zubia for about 700 m (0.4 miles) to a T-junction. Turn left at the T-junction.

Starting Point of the Wadi Zubia Forest Walk

Walk until you reach the main street of Zubia village. Cross the main road and go left. Turn immediately right into a street, then left, then right again while you walk towards the valley and a T-junction. You see the valley ahead of you with an asphalt road that runs parallel to the wadi at the T-junction. At this point, you leave the little town behind.

Facing the valley, turn left at the T-junction and after about 50 m (160 ft.), take the road into the valley on your right for 700 m (0.4 miles). After you have crossed the wadi through farm land, turn right and find your way up to the left through the trees. On top of the hill you will see more ruins. You are now near the parking area which is ahead of you.

Getting There *From Amman*

Drive from Amman in the direction of Jerash and Irbid on Route 35. Make a left turn onto Route 20 and follow directions to Ajloun. Make a right turn onto Route 55. In the center of Ajloun, reset your odometer and drive towards Irbid on Route 55 following the directions below.

From Ajloun

From the Ajloun Castle, drive to the city center and make a left turn at the traffic light at the T-junction. Reset your odometer and drive towards Irbid on Route 55 and initially follow the signs to the Ajloun Forest Reserve and Zubia. Do not turn off to the Ajloun Reserve. Continue driving north towards Irbid. After

11.9 km (7.4 miles) from Ajloun's city center, turn left at the traffic lights. Stay on the asphalt road for 3 km (1.9 miles) until you see a Y-junction. Take the left road and drive for another 1.6 km (1 mile) until you see a main asphalt road to the right. Do not turn right, but stay on the road for another 2.1 km (1.3 miles) and go right where it forks, then turn immediately right again after 100 m (300 ft.).

Drive straight uphill and do not turn right to the little settlement. Just follow the road and after 1.3 km (0.8 miles) you reach the parking area of Wadi Zubia. You are now south of the wadi while the town of Zubia is north of the wadi.

The starting point of the hike is not that easy to find, but you can download from *www.hiking-in-jordan.com* an E-trail with directions from the Ajloun Castle to Wadi Zubia. The file is "04-1 Driving Directions from Ajloun Castle to Wadi Zubia."

0:12	-	The parking area near the Roman ruins.
0:44	-	Not far from the ruins, you see an open field leading into the wadi that narrows with trees on your left and right.
0:50	-	Follow the trail while you find your way through the dense forest.
1:18	-	The service road leading to the town of Zubia.

Video Notes

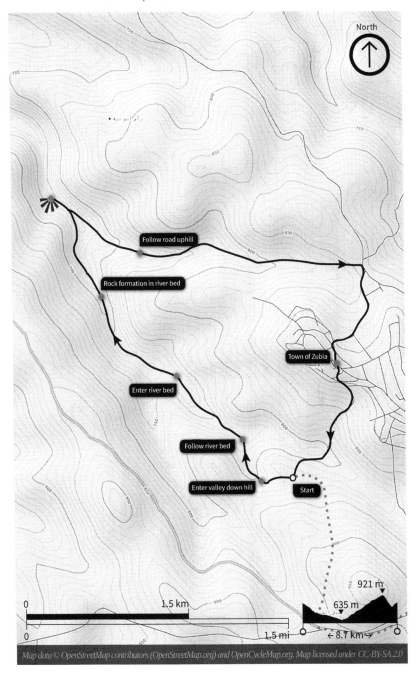

North

Follow road uphill

Rock formation in river bed

Town of Zubia

Enter river bed

Follow river bed

Enter valley down hill

Start

0   1.5 km

0   1.5 mi

921 m

635 m

← 8.7 km →

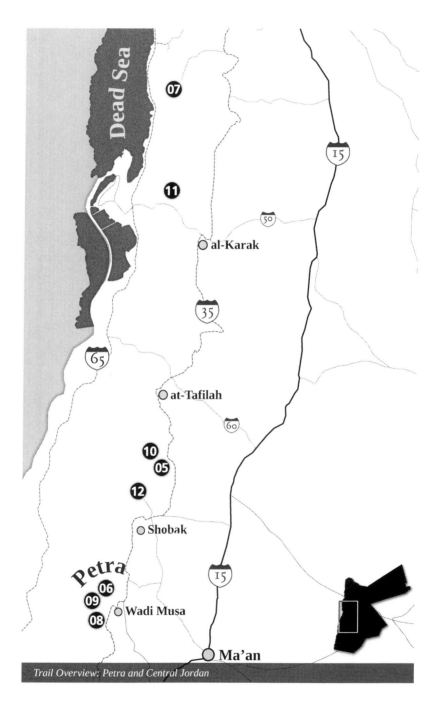

Trail Overview: Petra and Central Jordan

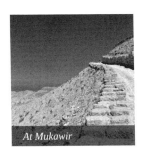
At Mukawir

Region
Petra and
Central Jordan

Dana Feynan Trail

05

Situated in the Dana Biosphere Reserve, the trail leads from Dana village towards Wadi Araba and the village of Feynan, south of the Dead Sea. The reserve is managed by the RSCN and is recognized by UNESCO as Jordan's first biosphere reserve. It contains different bio-geographical zones associated with the large range of elevations present in the reserve.

Introduction

The reserve's canyon is undoubtedly one of Jordan's most impressive natural formations. The views of the reserve from Dana village are truly magnificent. It

View from the Dana Lodge

is a fantastic hike into the canyons, especially if you organize a multi-day visit to the reserve to combine the Dana Feynan Trail with the nearby Wadi Ghuweir Trail to Feynan *(» page 112)*.

You need to be reasonably fit for this trail. Although it is easy to follow the path, we classify the trail as moderately difficult due to its length of 14 km (8.7 miles), 6-hour duration and the difference in elevation of 912 meters (2,992 ft.). A GPS device or guide is not required.

Trail Description

The trail starts in Dana village. Walk down the main street through the village past the few hotels down into the valley on a winding gravel road. After about 2 km (1.3 miles), the path levels. Continue walking following the path with the riverbed on your right for about 2 km (1.3 miles).

At this point, you have the option to go uphill or to continue to the right. Do not go uphill, but take the path to the right towards the wadi. After 130 meters (427 ft.), the path curves to the left and follows the wadi on your right.

	05 Dana Feynan Trail
Duration:	6 hours
Level:	Moderate
Starting Point Coordinates:	N30 40.457 E35 36.491
Starting Point:	Dana village.
Is a Four Wheel Drive Car Required?	A 4x4 car is not required. You can park a normal car in Dana village. If you start from Feynan, a 4x4 car is required (or you can use the Bedouin shuttle to Feynan arranged through the Feynan Eco Lodge).
Distance:	14 km (8.7 miles)
Highest Point:	1,228 m (4,029 ft.)
Lowest Point:	316 m (1,037 ft.)
Difference in Elevation:	912 m (2,992 ft.)
Trail Type:	Linear Trail (one way)
Is a GPS Device Required?	No
The Nearest Point with Amenities:	Hotels in the village of Dana and the RSCN Eco Lodge in Feynan.

After 1.8 km (1.1 miles), scramble up the little river bank when you cross a side stream of the wadi and follow the trail to your right, which continues to follow the wadi on your right. After 840 meters (0.5 miles), you reach a nice picnic area near a small stream with dense vegetation in the wadi. You are now just beyond the halfway point of the trail at 7.6 km (4.7 miles) from Dana village.

Follow the path for 2.9 km (1.8 miles) where you can either follow the wadi or stay on the path on the left that eventually will end up in the river bed. Either way, continue walking south-west until you reach the Feynan Eco Lodge in 2.6 km (1.6 miles).

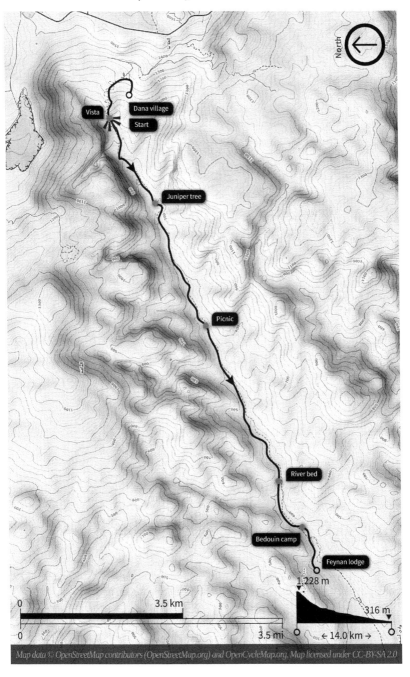

Vista
Dana village
Start
Juniper tree
Picnic
River bed
Bedouin camp
Feynan lodge
1,228 m
316 m

0   3.5 km
0   3.5 mi

← 14.0 km →

We could not find trail markers in the reserve, but by following the wadi straight downhill from Dana village, you will eventually end up near the Feynan Eco Lodge after approximately 6 hours.

Getting There

From Amman

Take the Desert Highway (Route 15) south for approximately 165 km (103 miles) from the 7th Circle in Amman passing the airport. After al-Husayniya village, look for exit signs to the Dana Biosphere Reserve and al-Qadisiya village, and follow the road to Dana.

Approximately 11 km (6.8 miles) from the Desert Highway exit, turn left to al-Qadisiya village. Towards the end of the village, follow a sign to Dana village on your left.

If you miss the turn-off, approximately 22 km (13.7 miles) from the Desert Highway exit, you will see the Rashadiyeh cement factory on your left. Continue for 1.3 km (0.8 miles) after the factory until you are at the King's Highway. Turn left at the junction and follow the signs to Dana village.

From Aqaba

Drive north on the Desert Highway (Route 15) for approximately 136 km (84.5 miles) from the customs check-point near Aqaba and follow the exit signs to the Dana Biosphere Reserve and al-Qadisiya village at the overpass.

Approximately 11 km (6.8 miles) from the Desert Highway exit, turn left to al-Qadisiya village. Towards the end of al-Qadisiya village, follow a sign to Dana village on your left.

If you miss the turn-off, approximately 22 km (13.5 miles) from the Desert Highway exit, you will see the Rashadiyeh cement factory on your left. Continue for 1.3 km (0.8 miles) after the factory until you are at the King's Highway. Turn left at the junction and follow the signs to Dana village.

About the Dana Biosphere Reserve

- The Dana Biosphere Reserve was established in the 1980s and is Jordan's largest biosphere reserve (320 km^2 or 123.5 miles^2). The reserve is comprised of a complex system of mountains and valleys.
- Renovations to the nearby Ottoman-era village of Dana are ongoing to develop the site as Jordan's first heritage village for eco-tourism.
- According to UNESCO, more than 800 plant and 449 animal species can be found within the biosphere reserve including several endangered animals such as the sand cat, the Syrian wolf, the lesser kestrel and the spiny-tailed lizard.
- About 100 archaeological sites have been found in the reserve. The area is believed to be one of the oldest continuously inhabited areas in the world, with remnants of Neolithic villages, ancient copper mines, Roman aqueducts and Byzantine churches.
- Wadi Feynan was an important copper ore mining area during Roman times. It is believed that copper ore mining came to an end in the later Byzantine period.
- The ruins at Feynan are not far from the Feynan Eco Lodge, the end point of the trail. Walk from the lodge on the access road towards the town of Feynan for 2.1 km (1.3 miles), with the dry river bed on your right. As you approach a large wadi (Wadi Ghuweir), you will see the ruins on your left.
- The reserve may be closed during Ramadan. Please check the RSCN website for the latest information on opening times.
- You pay the entrance fee to the reserve at the RSCN lodge in Dana village.

Logistics

- The RSCN Feynan and Dana lodges in the reserve cater to tourists with a healthy travel budget. If you cannot afford the lodges, you can visit the reserve for a day with no overnight if you have transport arranged at Feynan or Dana village to return to your car.
- Alternatively, if you like to stay overnight in Dana village in a budget hotel, you need to reverse the trail. You would start in Feynan, walk to Dana village, stay overnight and walk or drive back to

Feynan the next day.

- If you plan to eat dinner at the Feynan Eco Lodge, we recommend that you share your estimated time of arrival with the lodge's management if this is after 6 PM. They tend to serve dinner early.

Trail Notes

- The Dana Feynan Trail has the greatest elevation drop (912 m, 2,992 ft.) of all trails in our collection, starting from 1,228 meters (4,029 ft.) at Dana village to 316 meters (1,037 ft.) near the Feynan Eco Lodge.
- The RSCN permits you to hike this trail without a guide as it is a straightforward one way, 6-hour hike to the Feynan Eco Lodge. You will need to arrange for transport from Feynan to Dana village if you do not want to walk back the next day.
- It is 3 hours by car to return to Dana village from Feynan. Alternatively, you can combine the trail with the Wadi Ghuweir Trail to Feynan *(» page 112)* for a multi-day hiking adventure.

Video Notes

0:14	-	Dana village near the valley.
0:21	-	A view of the Dana Biosphere Reserve.
0:47	-	The historic village of Dana.
0:57	-	The starting point of the trail that leads into the Biosphere Reserve.
1:45	-	The path to Feynan is easy to follow.
2:35	-	The RSCN Feynan Eco Lodge.

06 Little Petra Canyon Trail

Introduction Little Petra (Bayda or al-Beidha) is a unique histori-cal site. Situated in the Siq al Barid (the cold Siq) near Petra in Wadi Musa, the area once was the "mountain suburb" of Petra and a stop for caravans on one of the many long trading routes that converged on Petra.

Here the cool of the Siq offered a place for weary travelers to eat, rest and do business in comfort. Little Petra was also a center for agricultural production with a complex of dams and cisterns that provided essential water.

You will see some of the dams and cisterns on this magnificent trail that leads through spectacular landscapes and rock formations. Rarely visited by tourists, this 4-hour, 6.9 km (4.3 miles) trail is spectacular and provides unparalleled views of the area. Anyone who is well prepared and reasonably fit can hike this trail. You need to be able to scramble up some boulders. A local guide or GPS device is required.

Trail Description From the car park, go past the shops. The first facade you encounter on the right is the Colonnaded Hall. Then you pass through a narrowing of the cliffs into Siq al Barid. It widens again, and on the left you can find a small cistern for water storage chiseled into the rock.

Further on, to the left, a narrow gully has ancient stone steps that lead up to the remains of a very old stone dam and a conduit carved into the rock.

GPS FILE	06 LITTLE PETRA CANYON TRAIL
Duration:	4 hours
Level:	Moderate
Starting Point Coordinates:	N30 22.618 E35 27.320
Starting Point:	The entrance to Little Petra.
Is a Four Wheel Drive Car Required?	A 4x4 car is not required. You can park a normal car near the entrance.
Distance:	6.9 km (4.3 miles)
Highest Point:	1,210 m (3,970 ft.)
Lowest Point:	1,035 m (3,397 ft.)
Difference in Elevation:	175 m (573 ft.)
Trail Type:	Circular Trail
Is a GPS Device Required?	Yes
The Nearest Point with Amenities:	You may find toilets and snacks near the entrance.

Continuing along the main path, the Siq narrows, then widens again revealing a number of carved rooms.

On the left is a large room with a cistern beside it, and just past these is the Painted Biclinium. You can walk up the well worn steps to look inside. There isn't much paint left, but check out the stone pillars with beautiful natural patterns in the rock. This is a good vantage point to see the remains of stairs on the opposite cliff.

Moving on, climb the eroded steps through a narrow and beautiful Siq. At the top you are likely to be rewarded with a cool breeze and a couple of trinket shops where you can rest in the shade, chat with the locals and drink tea. Once you have purchased all the snow domes you need, continue in the same

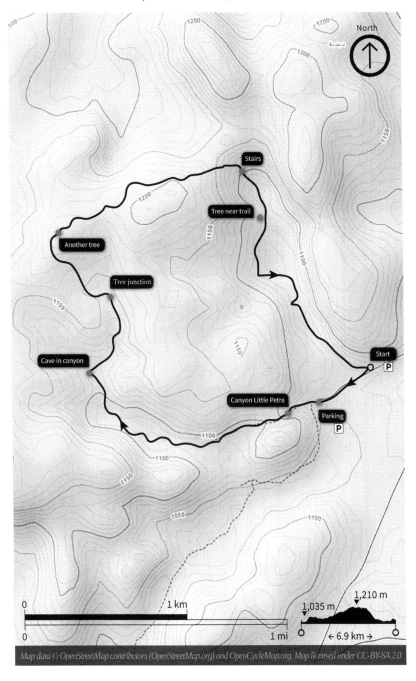

direction by descending a crack to the wadi below, where there is a huge juniper and a Kermes Oak, *Quercus calliprinos*.

Walk upstream (to the right) in the wadi bed, surrounded by rugged domes. There are more juniper and Kermes Oaks. You will pass several very old stone dams, further clues to the extent and sophistication of the methods to catch and control water in ancient times. In winter and spring, there will be masses of sea squill (*Urginea maritima*) on the gravel slopes. Look for paths just out of the soft wadi bed for easier walking.

About 700 m (0.4 miles) from where you entered this wadi is a larger stone dam, about 3 m (10 ft.) high. It is completely silted up with the debris of floods over the centuries. From here, walk along the right side of the wadi and head up the hill just before a steep-sided Siq that enters from the right.

Keep the Siq to your left. You'll come to a saddle; descend to the other side, turn left at the bottom to enter the Siq. Turn right and follow it up. There are many tough, old junipers and Kermes Oaks.

Keep to the main Siq until you come to a rocky wadi entering from the east (right), opposite a cave on the left. Follow this rocky wadi up for 100 m (328 ft.) until you are past a narrow Siq on the left, then clamber up the hill on your left. Go to a cleft between some boulders and continue climbing up heading north-east, keeping the Siq below you on the left all the time, finding the best path you can.

Look for a clump of trees where the main Siq comes to an abrupt end. Descend to just above this place, and turn right to follow a wadi bed which winds and climbs. Look for Blue Agama lizards here. You will pass a series of dams, all silted or washed out. The wadi curves to the north-west then peters out. Hold the line heading north-west to the top of domes, at first yellow, then rusty-brown.

On the Trail

You will reach the summit and be rewarded with exceptional views to the north and west. Continue north-east over the purple shingled top of the plateau, keeping nearby on your left a drop-off and after that a maze of domes. Stay on top holding this line. You will descend into a saddle and instead of making your way up the other side, pick a line around to the left, roughly maintaining your current contour.

Keep the Siq to the left in view, trending north-east, and look for a gully that will take you down to the north. It has a dark, steep-sided dome to the left of it. Exit this gully to the right just before some steep domes on your right. Keep the same eastern line, contouring below some more domes. When a cliff appears on your right, hug the base of it. Cross two gullies (the second with interesting hollowed rock formations) and head for a saddle 100 m (328 ft.) ahead of you with a small cleft beside a lone, almost dead Kermes Oak.

Pass the oak and descend the gully on the other side of the saddle, heading east. You will drop down into a sandy wadi leading south through a magnificent complex of domes. Follow this wadi down to the road. Turn right to return to your car.

If you have time (and any remaining energy), there is one more thing to look at before heading to your car. Turn left at the road from the parking area and continue for a few hundred meters to see an incongruous door in the side of a cliff. Have a peek in to see the mother of all cisterns.

Getting There

From Amman

It is a 245 km (152 mile) drive from Amman to Wadi Musa, in which vicinity Little Petra is located.

From the international airport in Amman, drive south on Route 15 (the Desert Highway), in the direction of Aqaba. Do not pass Ma'an, but turn right in the direction of Petra and Wadi Musa where signposted. Continue driving for 18.5 km (11.5 miles) and turn left in the direction of Petra. After 9 km (5.6 miles), follow the directions to Petra. It is difficult to miss.

From Aqaba

It is a 128 km (80 mile) drive to Petra on Route 15. The easiest, but slightly longer way is to drive to Ma'an. Pass Ma'an and turn right to the overpass in the direction of Petra and Wadi Musa. Continue driving for 18.5 km (11.5 miles) and turn left in the direction of Petra. After 9 km (5.6 miles), follow the directions to Petra. It is difficult to miss.

You can also drive to Petra following the King's Highway (Route 35).

From the Aqaba customs check-point on the Desert Highway (Route 15), drive north. After you have ascended from the valley, make a left turn onto Route 35 (the King's Highway) at the Rajif junction, 60 km (37 miles) from the customs check-point and follow the signs to Petra and Wadi Musa. This road can get snow in winter, so take care. Since this is a winding road, we recommend that you only drive this road during daylight. If you need to drive at night, we recommend that you drive to Ma'an and follow directions from there.

Continuing from both directions

Once in Wadi Musa, Little Petra is located 7.8 km (4.8 miles) north-west of the Petra visitors' center. From the visitors' center, take the road to the left (not into the main street in the center of Wadi Musa). This road curves to the left and you will see the parking lot for the buses on the left. After 420 m (0.3 miles), make a left turn and follow this curvy road for 7.4 km (4.6 miles). The road ends in a T-junction where you make a left turn to Little Petra. There are also signposts to al-Beidha to guide you in the right direction.

The Trail Starts at Little Petra

Diana Kirkbride, the British archaeologist who also worked on the discovery of the Nabatean Temple in Wadi Rum, excavated Little Petra in the 1950s and 1960s when she discovered a pre-pottery Neolithic B occupation. She also discovered Natufian hunting encampments with great quantities of bones from Bezoar goats and some Ibex. The Nabatean period dates back to the 1st and 2nd centuries BC.

- Apart from Little Petra itself, this complex trail is not marked and is difficult to follow solely using the trail description in the book.
- Do not hike this trail without either a GPS and spare batteries or a guide from the area. Do not attempt to hike alone. It is wise to go with a group.
- It is an isolated area with little mobile phone reception.
- Be aware that the entrance to Little Petra is often locked around sunset.
- Don't leave too late, to avoid hiking in the dark. We recommend that you build in a safety margin of at least one hour for the estimated time of arrival before sunset starts.
- This walk is mostly off track with some awkward clambering over rough terrain and plenty of hills.
- There is no marked hiking trail, although evidence of the passage of other people is apparent for much of the way.
- You need good shoes as there is some broken ground, but it is not steep.
- Care must be taken in the hiking area. You must be self-reliant. Don't expect a passer-by to assist as there are few visitors here.
- There is no rock climbing involved and no need for ropes if you pick the right path.

Video Notes

0:12	-	The shops at the entrance of Little Petra.
1:02	-	The gate to Little Petra.
1:25	-	The steps to the wadi.
2:30	-	The large stone dam in the wadi.
2:35	-	The cave.
2:55	-	On top of the hillside with exceptional views.

Petra and Central Jordan

07 Mukawir Mini Circuit

Introduction Explore the relatively unknown ruins of the Mukawir Fortress (Machaerus) with stunning panoramic views of the Dead Sea. The site is famous for Salome's Dance and John the Baptist's imprisonment and execution (beheading).

The archaeological site is being developed by the Jordanian Tourism Board and the Ministry of Tourism and Antiquities, and nowadays can be reached easily on a path leading to the top of the hillside. The visitors' center provides cold drinks and has toilets.

This mini circuit is one of the shortest walks in the collection. Although it takes 1.5 hours to walk the 1.1 km (0.7 miles) trail, the walk gives anyone a good workout walking uphill. The views are incredible and Mukawir's history make this unique place worth a visit. You do not need a guide or GPS device to complete this trail.

Trail Description Although Mukawir is located on top of a hill at an altitude of 699 meters (2,292 ft.), the difference in elevation on the walk uphill is only 56 meters (183 ft.). The path is well maintained and cannot be missed. After you have purchased your entrance ticket, walk from the visitors' center at the parking lot to the gate.

Walk down the steps and follow the path until you are on top of the hill. From this point, you can backtrack on the path you came from or follow the GPS trail that leads to the old path. The old path is certainly

GPS File	07 Mukawir Mini Circuit
Duration:	1.5 hours
Level:	Easy
Starting Point Coordinates:	N31 33.933 E35 37.646
Starting Point:	Mukawir visitors' center.
Is a Four Wheel Drive Car Required?	A 4x4 car is not required. You can park a normal car at the visitors' center.
Distance:	1.1 km (0.7 miles)
Highest Point:	699 m (2,292 ft.)
Lowest Point:	643 m (2,109 ft.)
Difference in Elevation:	56 m (183 ft.)
Trail Type:	Circular Trail
Is a GPS Device Required?	No
The Nearest Point with Amenities:	The visitors' center has toilets, a little shop and a restaurant.

less comfortable and more slippery, but gives you the opportunity to complete a mini circular trail instead of backtracking.

Getting There

From Madaba

Drive south on the King's Highway (Route 35) for 12.5 km (7.8 miles) until you reach the town of Libb. Make a right turn and follow the road for 21 km (13 miles) directly to the visitors' center of Mukawir.

From Amman/Aqaba

Starting at the 7th Circle in Amman, take Route 40 towards the Dead Sea for 45 km (28 miles) until it merges with the Dead Sea Highway (Route 65). Continue to drive south to the Panoramic Complex turn-off on your left. Make a left turn and drive uphill.

If you come from Aqaba, drive north on the Dead Sea Highway (Route 65). While driving north, you will

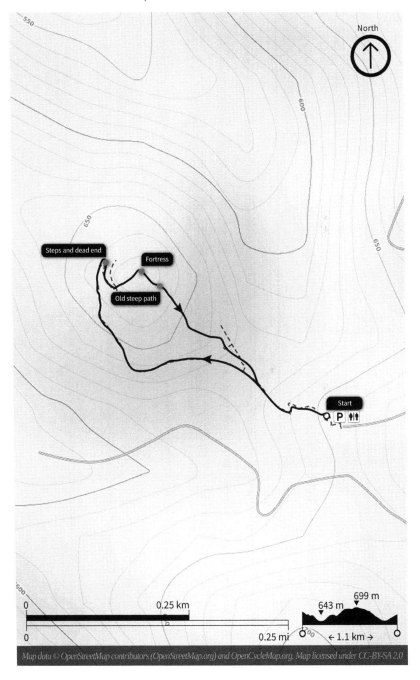

View of the Dead Sea

pass the towns or settlements of Rahma, Gharandal, Al Safi and Potash City. From the Mujib Bridge, continue to drive 21 km (13.4 miles) north and make a right turn onto the road towards the Panoramic Complex.

Continuing from both directions
Whether you come from the direction of Aqaba or Amman, after the Panoramic Complex turn-off, you will cross the Wadi Abu al-Asal Bridge and then a second bridge across Wadi Himara. This is the last bridge before the Panoramic Complex on your right.

Pass the Panoramic Complex and follow the signs to Hamamat Ma'in for 2.4 km (1.5 miles). Turn right and drive down a steep road into the valley until you reach the springs.

From this point, the road connects the Hamamat Ma'in Hot Springs with Mukawir. It is a beautiful drive through dramatic landscapes on steep slopes. From the lowest point in the valley, continue driv-

ing uphill for 8.4 km (5.2 miles) until you reach a T-junction. Turn right and follow the road through the mountains for 2 km (1.2 miles) to the visitors' center of Mukawir.

About Mukawir
- Mukawir was part of a group of fortified hillsides (including Masada) rebuilt by King Herod (Herod the Great). It was located at the southern border of Peraea near the territory of the King of Nabataea.
- Mukawir is similar to Masada in Israel in the sense that it was captured by a Roman garrison after it was occupied by Jewish rebels.
- It was recaptured by the Roman Commander Lucius Bassus after a seven month siege in 70 AD. You still can see the remnants of the siege ramp near the site (a large pile of rubble on the hillside).
- The Jewish rebels allegedly surrendered and the siege ramp was never used.
- Most of the site has not been excavated. When you are on top of the hill, you basically walk on the roofs of the buildings that are buried under sand.

- The historian Josephus described Mukawir (Machaerus) in Antiquitates Judaicae XVIII 5,2 as a palace where John the Baptist was imprisoned for 2 years before he was beheaded in 32 AD.
- Herod Antipas (the son of Herod the Great) ordered the imprisonment of John the Baptist for two reasons:
  - First, Herodias was married to Herod Antipas' brother before she divorced him to marry Herod Antipas. John the Baptist criticized her divorce.
  - To make things even worse, John the Baptist also publicly criticized Herod Antipas' marriage to Herodias.
- Salome was Herodias' daughter from her first marriage.
- During Herod Antipas' birthday party at Mukawir, Salome danced for her new step-father (Herod Antipas) who was so pleased that he promised her anything she wanted. She asked at the instigation of her mother Herodias for the beheading of John the Baptist and the rest is history.

Mukawir, Salome's Dance and John the Baptist's Beheading

- The Hamamat Ma'in hot Springs are near to Mukawir.
- Mukawir does not receive as much traffic as other historical sites in Jordan, but provides equally stunning or even better views of the Dead Sea than Mount Nebo and is less crowded.
- You can see the lights of al-Quds (Jerusalem) and Ariha (Jericho) on a clear night.

Trail Notes

0:19	-	Mukawir on top of the hillside with the Dead Sea in the distance.
0:25	-	The parking lot near the entrance.
0:37	-	The gate leading to the path to the hillside.
1:16	-	Magnificent views of the Dead Sea.
1:19	-	On top of the hillside at Mukawir.

Video Notes

Steps to Mukawir

Petra High Place of Sacrifice Trail

08

This stunning trail leads through one of the new Seven Wonders of the World, Petra in Jordan. As you follow the trail, rediscover Petra as Johann Ludwig Burckhardt did in 1812 when Petra was introduced to the Western World.

Introduction

While walking on the trail, you will see a large number of monuments in Petra including the Treasury, the High Place of Sacrifice and the Obelisks, the Lion Monument, the Garden Temple, the Roman Soldier Tomb, the Renaissance Tomb and the Monastery; more monuments than most tourists see.

You need to plan for a full day of hiking to complete this trail. With a distance of 17.5 km (10.9 miles) and duration of 8 hours, this is a more demanding hike than the alternative Petra Monastery Trail (» page 90).

You do not need a guide or GPS device with our E-trail to find the High Place of Sacrifice and later on the Monastery. You can always backtrack on the trail from the Monastery if you do not have a GPS, as using a GPS or guide is recommended after the Monastery.

Walking through the Siq to the Treasury **Trail Description**
(2.7 km, 1.7 miles)

From the main entrance to Petra, walk through the Great Siq, observing the water conduits chiseled into the cliffs. At the end of the Great Siq, 2.7 km (1.7 miles) from the visitors' center, you will be greeted

GPS FILE	08 PETRA HIGH PLACE OF SACRIFICE TRAIL
Duration:	8 hours
Level:	Moderate
Starting Point Coordinates:	N30 19.622 E35 28.078
Starting Point:	Petra visitors' center.
Is a Four Wheel Drive Car Required?	A 4x4 car is not required. You can park a normal car at the visitors' center.
Distance:	17.5 km (10.9 miles)
Highest Point:	1,102 m (3,616 ft.)
Lowest Point:	852 m (2,796 ft.)
Difference in Elevation:	250 m (820 ft.)
Trail Type:	Circular Trail
Is a GPS Device Required?	A GPS device or guide is recommended after you have reached the Monastery.
The Nearest Point with Amenities:	Public toilets and various restaurants are located inside Petra.

by the extraordinary sight of al-Khazneh ("The Treasury") carved into the cliff.

Turn right at al-Khazneh to follow the wadi bed down past the tombs and trinket stalls. About 300 m (984 ft.) from al-Khazneh, and immediately after the toilets on the left, there is a sign on the left pointing the way up stairs to the High Place of Sacrifice. If you come to the Roman-style theater you have gone too far.

Taking the Steps to the Obelisks and the High Place of Sacrifice (1.1 km, 0.7 miles)
From the start the magnificent, ancient carved stairs quickly gain you fine views of the wadi and tombs below. The stairs climb relentlessly up Wadi al-Mahfur, switching from one side of the wadi to the other. When you pause to catch your breath,

take time to observe the chisel marks up the cliffs revealing how much stone had to be removed to create the set of stairs on which you are improving your cardio-vascular fitness. The steps reveal the wear of countless pairs of feet having passed this way over the millennia. There are a few trinket shops on the way. Don't be shy about accepting offers of tea and a rest; it is a courtesy and there is no obligation that you buy anything. Simply be courteous in return.

At the head of the wadi, where there are more trinket shops, turn right between two large rocks and continue on up. After a couple more minutes, near the top, you will come to an intersection near a tea shop. The trail up to the right (north) leads past the remains of what must have been an enormous building (possibly a crusader fort) to the top of the mountain (al-Nejr) and the High Place of Sacrifice. Up to the left are two obelisks.

At the High Place of Sacrifice

Firstly, check out the High Place of Sacrifice to the right. Follow the steps up to the carved pools and sacrificial font of the High Place of Sacrifice. Be sure to walk to the north end of the ridge for magnificent views of the ruins of the city of Petra below.

After you have taken your photos, wander back down to the junction. Before continuing on the trail (which continues south, straight past the shop), the obelisks are well worth a look. They are impressive, but even more so when you appreciate these monuments are made of solid rock and were created by chiseling away the top of the mountain.

Continuing the Trail into Wadi al-Farasa
(1 km, 0.6 miles)

Continuing on the trail south, the track cuts back to the right and zigzags down the hill. This was a processional way to the High Place of Sacrifice and is both a beautiful walk and a great escape from the crowds. Keep a look out for the beautiful Blue Agama lizard and the Sinai Agama (*Pseudotrapelus sinaitus*) along here. A good place to look for them is at a

The Treasury

lookout where walkers have taken it upon themselves to build myriads of little stone cairns.

As you continue to descend to Wadi al-Farasa, you pass a few tough junipers clinging to the cliffs and get views of tombs across the valley.

Stop for a rest at the Lion Monument, where water conduits carved into the stone once channeled water down to the head of a large carved lion, and presumably the water once poured from its mouth into a pool. It must have been a beautiful place. The steps onwards are steep, but the stonework magnificent. Take time to appreciate the rainbow colors in many of the cliffs here.

Below this is a valley with numerous tombs and stunning rainbow-colored cliffs. Look for where the stone has freshly broken away to reveal the true vividness of the rock beneath. As you get to the valley bottom you pass the Soldier Tomb, well worth a look inside, and several other tombs. If you have time, explore them all.

Ahead of you is the Garden Hall, which was once supplied by water from a dam to the right (which appears to be simply a stone wall). Inside the Garden Hall is an impressive skylight cut through 2 m (6.5 ft.) of stone.

From the Garden Hall to the Junction (480 m, 0.3 miles)
Continue on the trail in the valley bottom. You come to a junction, where you can go straight on north then north-west to the museum, restaurants and steps to the Monastery. You can also go right to cut straight back towards the Royal Tombs near the Roman-style theater on a trail that skirts around the foot of the mountain al-Nejr.

Either way, find your way to the restaurants near the steps to the Monastery after 950 m (0.6 miles).

730 steps to the Monastery
(1.4 km, 0.9 miles)

From the restaurants, follow the main track heading north towards the Monastery.

At the bottom of the steps to the Monastery, there is a short detour to the left that takes you to the Lion Triclinium. The hike to the Monastery can be hard work, especially on a hot day. There are plenty of trinkets shops where you can grab a cup of tea and places selling food and drinks on the way and at the Monastery.

The 730 steps are calculated as the sum of steps going up minus the few steps going down while you walk towards the Monastery.

Walking Past the Monastery to the Junction
(2.3 km, 1.4 miles)

From the Monastery, walk on with the Monastery and mountain to your right. You will find yourself on a trail leading down a gully to begin with, but you need to cut off to the right over rocks very soon. This is where it becomes tricky finding your way to the trail and where a GPS device or guide is certainly useful.

From here the path is less clear and suddenly it is very isolated. This is a good moment to make a decision whether you want to continue the trail or head back the way you came. From this point forward, we recommend that you use the GPS trail that comes with the book unless you have arranged an experienced guide.

Keep the cliff to your right, and aim for a pass at the base of the cliff. The trail is used by Bedouins, but unmarked. Stay up high above a few junipers near the cliff and skirt around the mountain. You are immediately rewarded with absolutely magnificent views to the west and north into Wadi Araba. Take care at the exposed section.

After about 20 minutes you come to steps and a man-made path. You descend and re-ascend around 200 steps. This area is quiet with plenty of viewpoints. About an hour from the Monastery you come to a junction.

The Monastery

From the Junction to the Restaurants
(2.1 km, 1.3 miles)

The trail back to the restaurants near the steps to the Monastery follows a path to the right, down a valley of tombs heading south-east.

To the Visitors' Center from the Restaurants
(4.3 km, 2.7 miles)

From the restaurants near the steps to the Monastery, simply follow the main track through the Colonnaded Street and the Facades Street with many tombs, all worthy of exploration, and arrive through the Siq back at the visitors' center.

From Amman   Getting There

It is a 245 km (152 mile) drive from Amman to Wadi Musa where Petra is located. We recommend that you arrive a day before you explore Petra. This gives you the opportunity to start early in the morning, because you will need a full day to complete the trail.

From the international airport in Amman, drive south on Route 15 (the Desert Highway), in the direction of Aqaba. Do not pass Ma'an, but turn right in the direction of Petra and Wadi Musa where signposted. Continue driving for 18.5 km (11.5 miles) and turn left in the direction of Petra. After 9 km (5.6 miles), follow the directions to Petra. It is difficult to miss.

From Aqaba

It is a 128 km (80 mile) drive from Aqaba to Wadi Musa and Petra. You could leave Aqaba around 5 AM to have an early start and avoid a night in Wadi Musa. We recommend that you arrive the day before to allow plenty of time to explore Petra.

The easiest, but slightly longer way is to drive to Ma'an and follow the directions to Petra and Wadi Musa as described above.

You can also drive to Petra following the King's Highway (Route 35).

From the Aqaba customs check-point on the Desert

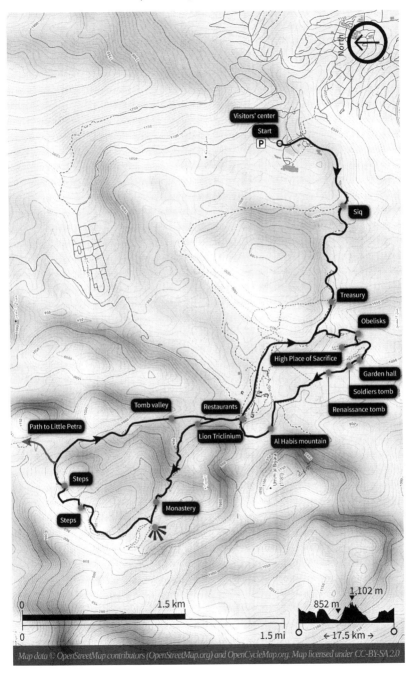

Visitors' center

Start

P

Siq

Treasury

Obelisks

High Place of Sacrifice

Garden hall

Soldiers tomb

Renaissance tomb

Tomb valley

Restaurants

Path to Little Petra

Lion Triclinium

Al Habis mountain

Steps

Monastery

Steps

North

0   1.5 km

0   1.5 mi

1,102 m

852 m

← 17.5 km →

Highway (Route 15), drive 60 km (37 miles) north and make a left turn at the Rajif Junction after you have climbed your way up from the valley. From the junction you are on Route 35 (the King's Highway). Follow the signposts to Petra. This road can get snow in winter, so take care. Since this is a winding road, we recommend that you only drive this during daylight. If you need to drive at night, we recommend that you drive to Ma'an and follow directions from there.

Trail Notes

- In winter, this can be a cold hike. Check the weather and be prepared.
- You do not need a guide or GPS device with our E-trail to find the High Place of Sacrifice and later on the Monastery.
- You can always backtrack down the trail once you have reached the High Place of Sacrifice and later on the Monastery.
- A GPS device or guide is recommended for the remainder of the trail after you have reached the Monastery.
- The Bedouin community has widened the trail at N30 20.574 E35 25.691.
- Do not lose your ticket to Petra. You may be asked to present the ticket when you return to Petra through the tomb valley.
- If you hike from Little Petra to Petra, make sure you have a valid ticket to Petra.

Video Notes

0:21	The start of the great Siq in Petra.
1:10	Al-Khazneh ("The Treasury") carved into the cliff.
1:40	Start of the trail to the High Place of Sacrifice.
2:33	The Obelisks.
2:42	At the High Place of Sacrifice.
3:10	Wadi al-Farasa.
3:38	The Soldiers Tomb and the Garden Hall.
4:07	The Renaissance Tomb.
4:19	View over the Facade Street.
4:53	One of the restaurants near the steps to the Monastery.
5:06	The steps to the Monastery are well maintained.
5:16	The Monastery.

The Mosaics in Petra

Petra High Place of Sacrifice Trail to Little Petra

General Description

We have two alternative E-trail routes to Little Petra through the High Place of Sacrifice. *The Petra High Place of Sacrifice Trail to Little Petra Route 1* is approximately 1 km (0.6 miles) longer in distance, but guides you to more monuments in the center of Petra before heading to the Monastery and Little Petra. Alternatively, the *Petra High Place of Sacrifice Trail to Little Petra Route 2* leads you further from tourist areas in the direction of al-Habis Mountain and the restaurants near the steps to the Monastery with more nature and space.

Either way, walk past the Monastery to the junction following the description of the Petra High Place of Sacrifice Trail. At the junction, about one hour from the Monastery, the trail back to the restaurants near the steps to the Monastery follows a path to the right, down a valley of tombs heading south-east. The trail to Little Petra follows a rough vehicle track to the left, heading north. It is 5.8 km (3.6 miles) from this point to Little Petra.

To walk to Little Petra, take the track to the north-east that meanders generally north up a wadi and out of the mountains. When you exit the wadi, a few hundred meters to the north is a free-standing rock formation. Follow the track that goes to the left and skirt around it by going right when you intersect another track. Follow this track.

The track skirts a gully to your left before turning north-east again. Follow the track in this general

GPS FILE	08-1 PETRA HIGH PLACE OF SACRIFICE TRAIL TO LITTLE PETRA	08-2 PETRA HIGH PLACE OF SACRIFICE TRAIL TO LITTLE PETRA
Duration:	8.5 hours	8 hours
Level:	Moderate	Moderate
Starting Point Coordinates:	N30 19.622 E35 28.078	N30 19.622 E35 28.078
Starting Point:	Petra visitors' center.	Petra visitors' center.
Is a Four Wheel Drive Car Required?	A 4x4 car is not required. You can park a normal car at the visitors' center.	A 4x4 car is not required. You can park a normal car at the visitors' center.
Distance:	17.9 km (11.1 miles)	16.7 km (10.4 miles)
Highest Point:	1,108 m (3,635 ft.)	1,102 m (3,616 ft.)
Lowest Point:	831 m (2,727 ft.)	856 m (2,807 ft.)
Difference in Elevation:	277 m (908 ft.)	246 m (809 ft.)
Trail Type:	Linear Trail (one way)	Linear Trail (one way)
Is a GPS Device Required?	A GPS device or guide is recommended after you have reached the Monastery. You do not need a guide or GPS device with our E-trail to find the High Place of Sacrifice and later on the Monastery. You can always backtrack down the trail once you have reached the Monastery nearly halfway along the trail.	A GPS device or guide is recommended after you have reached the Monastery. You do not need a guide or GPS device with our E-trail to find the High Place of Sacrifice and later on the Monastery. You can always backtrack down the trail once you have reached the Monastery nearly halfway along the trail.
The Nearest Point with Amenities:	Public toilets and various restaurants are located inside Petra.	Public toilets and various restaurants are located inside Petra.

direction as you approach a large rock massif on your left. Approximately 1 km (0.6 miles) from the gully you will be walking on the eastern side of the massif, with the road from Wadi Musa now on your right. Turn north when you round the eastern side of the massive to be at the Little Petra car park in less than 1 km (0.6 miles).

Keep in mind that you need to arrange transportation ahead of time from Little Petra back to Wadi Musa.

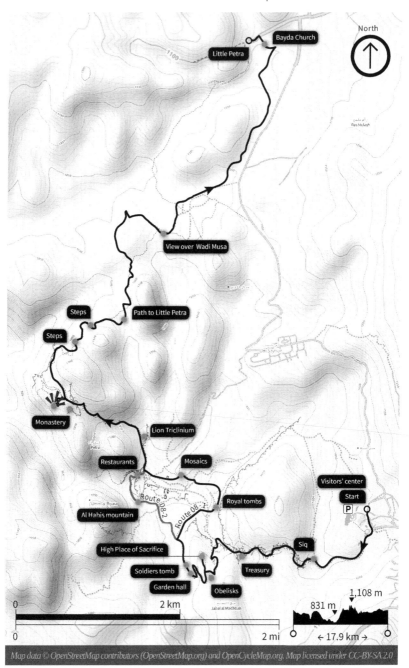

Gregory Shooting Videos on the Trail Past the Monastery

Trail

Petra Monastery Trail

09

This wonderful trail leads to a large number of sites in Petra including the Treasury, the Facades Street, the Grand Temple, the Mosaics and the Monastery. After you have navigated the 730 steps up to the Monastery, the trail continues through breathtaking landscapes and magnificent valleys. Alternatively, you may decide to head back directly to the restaurants near the steps to the Monastery. You do not need a guide or GPS device with our E-trail to find the Monastery.

Introduction

This is an easier hike than the High Place of Sacrifice Trail *(» page 76)* in Petra since it is 1.9 km (1.2 miles) shorter and more importantly, you need to

View of the Street of Facades

navigate significantly fewer steps.

Inevitably, by hiking this trail, you will see fewer monuments in Petra, but you will be able to spend more time in the center of Petra and the hike is overall less strenuous.

Trail Description   *Walking through the Siq to the Treasury*
(2.7 km, 1.7 miles)
From the main entrance to Petra, walk through the Great Siq, observing the water conduits chiseled into the cliffs. At the end of the Great Siq, 2.7 km (1.7 miles) from the visitors' center, you will be greeted by the extraordinary sight of al-Khazneh ("The Treasury") carved into the cliff.

Turn right at al-Khazneh to follow the Facades Street past the tombs and trinket stalls. You pass the Roman-style theater on your left and the Royal Tombs on your right. The trail leads up to the church with the mosaics before you arrive at the restaurants near the steps to the Monastery. While you walk down the trail towards the restaurants after viewing the mosaics, you will see the Colonnaded Street on the left down in the valley.

GPS FILE	09 PETRA MONASTERY TRAIL
Duration:	7 hours
Level:	Moderate
Starting Point Coordinates:	N30 19.622 E35 28.078
Starting Point:	Petra visitors' center.
Is a Four Wheel Drive Car Required?	A 4x4 car is not required. You can park a normal car at the visitors' center.
Distance:	15.6 km (9.7 miles)
Highest Point:	1,119 m (3,670 ft.)
Lowest Point:	852 m (2,796 ft.)
Difference in Elevation:	267 m (874 ft.)
Trail Type:	Circular Trail
Is a GPS Device Required?	A GPS device or guide is recommended after you have reached the Monastery. You do not need a guide or GPS device with our E-trail to find the Monastery. You can always backtrack down the trail once you have reached the Monastery nearly halfway along the trail.
The Nearest Point with Amenities:	Public toilets and various restaurants are located inside Petra.

Alternatively, you can stay on the Facades Street and walk straight on the Colonnaded Street to the restaurants bypassing the trail to the church and its mosaics.

730 Steps to the Monastery
(1.4 km, 0.9 miles)

From the restaurants near the steps to the Monastery, follow the main track heading north towards the Monastery. You will be accosted by touts trying to convince you to ride a donkey up to the Monastery. At the bottom of the steps to the Monastery, there is a short detour to the left that takes you to the Lion Triclinium.

Continue up the 730-odd steps past trinket stalls and mercenary drinks-vendors until you are suddenly on the top with the extraordinary Monastery on your right. Once you see someone in the "doorway" you realize how massive this façade really is. After you take your photos, it is really worth heading to the high point on the hill over to the left. This gives you a fantastic view of the Monastery and the wild landscape around it.

Walking Past the Monastery to the Junction (2.3 km, 1.4 miles)

From the Monastery, walk on with the Monastery and mountain to your right. You will find yourself on a trail leading down a gully to begin with, but you need to cut off to the right over rocks very soon. This is where it becomes tricky finding your way to the trail and where a GPS device or guide is certainly useful.

From here the path is less clear and suddenly it is very isolated. This is a good moment to make a decision whether you want to continue the trail or head back the way you came. From this point forward, we recommend that you use the GPS trail that comes with this book unless you have arranged an experienced guide.

Keep the cliff to your right and aim for a pass at the base of the cliff. The trail is used by Bedouins, but unmarked. Stay up high above a few junipers near the cliff and skirt around the mountain. You are immediately rewarded with absolutely magnificent views to the west and north into Wadi Araba. Take care at the exposed section.

After about 20 minutes you come to steps and a man-made path. You descend and re-ascend around 200 steps. This area is quiet with plenty of viewpoints. About an hour from the Monastery you come to a junction.

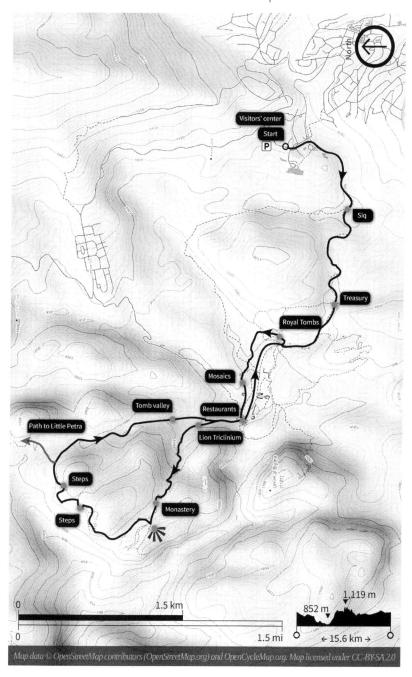

Visitors' center
Start
P
Siq
Treasury
Royal Tombs
Mosaics
Tomb valley
Restaurants
Path to Little Petra
Lion Triclinium
Steps
Steps
Monastery

North

0   1.5 km
0   1.5 mi

1,119 m
852 m
← 15.6 km →

From the Junction to the Restaurants (2.1 km, 1.3 miles)

The trail back to the restaurants near the steps to the Monastery follows a path to the right, down a valley of tombs heading south-east.

To the Visitors' Center from the Restaurants (4.3 km, 2.7 miles)

From the restaurants near the steps to the Monastery, simply follow the main track up through the Colonnaded Street and the Facades Street with many tombs, all worthy of exploration, and arrive through the Siq back at the visitors' center.

Getting There See Petra High Place of Sacrifice Trail (» page 76).

Trail Notes
- You do not need a guide or GPS device with our E-trail to find the Monastery.
- You can always backtrack down the trail once you have reached the Monastery.
- A GPS device or guide is recommended for the remainder of the trail after you have reached the Monastery.
- In winter, this can be a cold hike. Check the weather and be prepared.
- Do not lose your ticket to Petra. You may be asked to present the ticket when you return to Petra through the tomb valley.
- If you hike from Little Petra to Petra, make sure you have a valid ticket to Petra.
- The Bedouin community has widened the trail at N30 20.574 E35 25.691.

Video Notes

0:46	-	The great Siq in Petra.
0:59	-	Al-Khazneh ("The Treasury") carved into the cliff.
1:35	-	The Urn Tomb.
1:53	-	The mosaics not far from the restaurants near the steps to the Monastery.
2:20	-	The steps to the Monastery are well maintained.
2:42	-	The Monastery.
3:00	-	Bedouin camp near the trail.

Petra and Central Jordan

Petra Monastery Trail to Little Petra

Trail

09+

General Description

You can also walk from the Monastery to Little Petra, which is 800 m (0.5 miles) shorter than walking back to the visitors' center. Walk past the Monastery to the junction following the description of the Petra Monastery Trail. At the junction, about one hour from the Monastery, the trail back to the restaurants near the steps to the Monastery and museum follows a path to the right, down a valley of tombs heading south-east. The trail to Little Petra follows a rough vehicle track to the left, heading north. It is 5.8 km

A Panoramic View of Little Petra

(3.6 miles) from this point to Little Petra.

To walk to Little Petra, take the track to the north-east that meanders generally north up a wadi and out of the mountains. When you exit the wadi, a few hundred meters to the north is a free-standing rock formation. Follow the track that goes to the left and skirt around it by going right when you intersect another track. Follow this track.

The track skirts a gully to your left before turning north-east again. Follow the track in this general direction as you approach a large rock massif on your left. Approximately 1 km (0.6 miles) from the gully you will be walking on the eastern side of the massif, with the road from Wadi Musa now on your right. Turn north when you round the eastern side of the massive to be at the Little Petra car park in less than 1 km (0.6 miles).

Keep in mind that you need to arrange transportation ahead of time from Little Petra back to Wadi Musa.

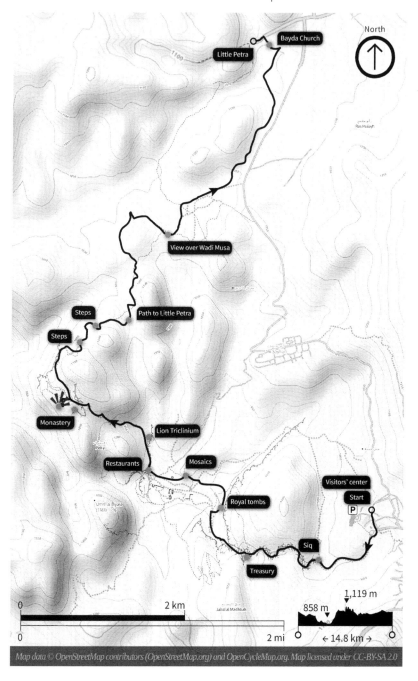

North

Bayda Church
Little Petra

Ras Mulayh

View over Wadi Musa

Steps
Path to Little Petra

Steps

Monastery

Lion Triclinium

Restaurants

Mosaics

Visitors' center

Start
P

Royal tombs

Siq

Treasury

0 ——— 2 km
0 ——— 2 mi

1,119 m
858 m
← 14.8 km →

GPS FILE	09-1 PETRA MONASTERY TRAIL TO LITTLE PETRA
Duration:	7.5 hours
Level:	Moderate
Starting Point Coordinates:	N30 19.622 E35 28.078
Starting Point:	Petra visitors' center.
Is a Four Wheel Drive Car Required?	A 4x4 car is not required. You can park a normal car at the visitors' center.
Distance:	14.8 km (9.2 miles)
Highest Point:	1,119 m (3,670 ft.)
Lowest Point:	858 m (2,815 ft.)
Difference in Elevation:	261 m (855 ft.)
Trail Type:	Linear Trail (one way)
Is a GPS Device Required?	A GPS device or guide is recommended after you have reached the Monastery. You do not need a guide or GPS device with our E-trail to find the Monastery. You can always backtrack down the trail once you have reached the Monastery nearly halfway along the trail.
The Nearest Point with Amenities:	Public toilets and various restaurants are located inside Petra.

Rummana Mountain Trail

10

Trail

This trail starts from the Dana Reserve's Rummana campground, not far away from Dana village. The campground has tents, a Bedouin tent for a sitting area, toilets, shower and gift shop. This walk is fantastic in spring when the flowers are out, but the views are stunning at any time.

Introduction

Although the circular trail is just 3.5 km (2.2 miles) measured from the campground, you need to be prepared to walk up to the top at 1,350 m (4,429 ft.) with a difference in elevation of 187 m (615 ft.). The trail is nevertheless easy to walk. You do not need a GPS device or guide to navigate Rummana.

From the visitors' center, take the little truck that ferries campers. Once at the Rummana campground, the trail starts on the right as you enter the camp. The trail takes you through sandstone domes with plenty of juniper trees. Look for the pistachio trees. They have very green leaves with seven pinnae (sub-leaves), red berries and corky bark. The trail soon turns north-west up the slope and becomes steeper.

Trail Description

There are rock cairns to mark the way. You may want to keep an eye on these because the trail is not clear at times. As you gain altitude, you get a fine view of the campground below and, further on, of the valley down towards Feynan.

Once on top of Rummana, after 1.4 km (0.9 miles) from the campground, you can return by the same way you came or walk a circuit that joins a track for

GPS FILE	10 RUMMANA MOUNTAIN TRAIL
Duration:	2 hours
Level:	Easy
Starting Point Coordinates:	N30 41.269 E35 34.366
Starting Point:	Campground in Dana Nature Reserve.
Is a Four Wheel Drive Car Required?	A 4x4 car is not required. You can park a normal car at the visitors' center.
Distance:	3.5 km (2.2 miles)
Highest Point:	1,350 m (4,429 ft.)
Lowest Point:	1,163 m (3,814 ft.)
Difference in Elevation:	187 m (615 ft.)
Trail Type:	Circular Trail
Is a GPS Device Required?	No
The Nearest Point with Amenities:	The campground and visitors' center have toilets.

4X4 cars after 800 m (0.5 miles). Turn right at the track and start your gradual descent in the direction of the campground. You will shortly be back at the campground. You can grab the shuttle-truck to save yourself the walk up the hill to the visitors' center.

Getting There *From Amman*
Take the Desert Highway (Route 15) south for approximately 165 km from the 7th Circle in Amman past the airport. As you pass al-Husayniya village, you will see an overpass preceded by exit signs to the Dana Biosphere Reserve and al-Qadisiya village. Take a right at this exit and follow the signs to Dana village.

From Aqaba
Drive north on the Desert Highway (Route 15) for approximately 136 km (84.4 miles) from the customs check-point near Aqaba. Follow the exit signs to the

Dana Biosphere Reserve and al-Qadisiya village by exiting right to the overpass before al-Husayniya village. Follow the signs to Dana village.

Continuing from both directions

Approximately 22 km (13.5 miles) from the Desert Highway exit, you will find the Rashadiyeh cement factory on your left. Continue to the junction with the King's Highway for 1.3 km (0.8 miles) after the factory. Turn right at the junction and follow the signs to the camp.

Trail Notes

- The RSCN Rummana campground caters to tourists with a relatively healthy travel budget. If you cannot afford to stay overnight at the campground, you can always visit the reserve for just a day.
- If you have your own tent and are self-reliant, at a pinch you can camp by the road outside the reserve. Otherwise go for a hotel in Dana village if you do not want to stay at the campground.
- The campground and reserve are open from March 1 to October 31. Please check the RSCN website for the latest information on opening times.

Video Notes

0:22	-	View over the Dana Nature Reserve.
0:52	-	The Rummana campground.
1:00	-	The Cave Trail as part of the extended version of the hike.
1:10	-	The road to the campground.
1:23	-	The trail on Rummana.

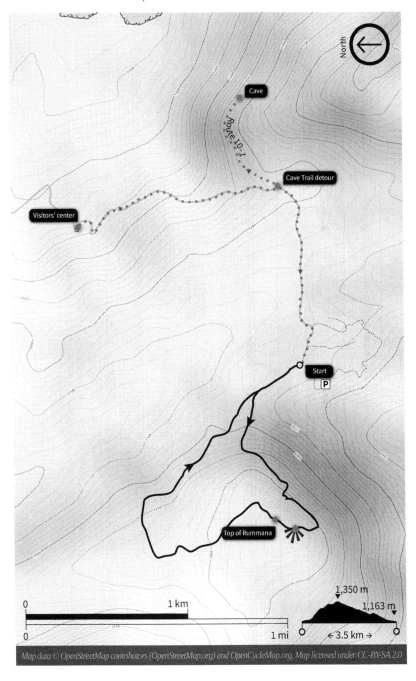

From the visitors' center, you can walk to the campground. The walk is downhill, takes 30 minutes and is worth the additional 3.6 km (2.2 miles) one way to the trail. From the reception, head down the hill on the road. After about 1 km (0.6 miles) you will see a sign to the Cave Trail on the left. Follow the trail along the escarpment for a few hundred meters to some caves. You could continue to find your way through to Dana village, but that hike is not described here.

Extended Alternative Version

Return to the main road to arrive at the campground. You pass planted woodland of Aleppo Pine and Phoenician Juniper on the way. Keep a look out for long-legged buzzards. At times, you get good numbers of them circling here. Once at the Rummana campground, follow the previous trail description.

GPS File	10-1 Rummana Mountain Trail and Cave Trail
Duration:	3.5 hours
Level:	Easy
Starting Point Coordinates:	N30 41.837 E35 34.793
Starting Point:	Dana Reserve visitors' center.
Is a Four Wheel Drive Car Required?	A 4x4 car is not required. You can park a normal car at the visitors' center.
Distance:	7.1 km (4.4 miles)
Highest Point:	1,376 m (4,515 ft.)
Lowest Point:	1,163 m (3,814 ft.)
Difference in Elevation:	213 m (701 ft.)
Trail Type:	Circular Trail
Is a GPS Device Required?	No
The Nearest Point with Amenities:	The campground and visitors' center have toilets.

11 Wadi Bin Hammad Tropical Rain Forest Trail

Introduction The Wadi Bin (Ibn) Hammad Hot Spring is situated between Madaba and al-Karak, south of the capital Amman. It is hidden deep inside a large valley with lush vegetation, hanging gardens, palm trees, and plenty of water running through a narrow gorge (Siq). The area is popular with locals because of the hot spring, cool temperatures and picnic opportunities.

This short and attractive family-friendly walk is an easy stroll for all ages. With just 4 km (2.5 miles) of walking to be done through the wadi round-trip, the trail is a wonderful introduction to Jordan's hidden natural treasures. The drive to the wadi on the valley's steep slopes is spectacular by itself, with magnificent views of the area.

To enjoy this beautiful walk you do not need any special equipment. A guide or GPS device is not required. Make sure you bring an extra pair of socks and shoes, because your feet will be wet.

Trail Description From the visitors' center, walk down the steps and enter the wadi. Do not cross the little bridge that leads to the hot springs. In the wadi, the gorge narrows gradually, while you walk through warm water on an easy to navigate bed of stones and boulders. Hanging gardens and waterfalls on either side of the gorge give you a refreshing taste of this oasis in the middle of a dramatic landscape with palm trees and ferns. The contrast with the dry cliffs cannot be greater.

Follow the wadi until it narrows into a Siq. The tem-

GPS FILE	11 WADI BIN HAMMAD TROPICAL RAIN FOREST TRAIL
Duration:	1.5 hours
Level:	Easy
Starting Point Coordinates:	N31 18.071 E35 37.867
Starting Point:	Wadi Bin Hammad visitors' center.
Is a Four Wheel Drive Car Required?	A 4x4 car is not required. You can park a normal car at the visitors' center.
Distance:	4.0 km (2.5 miles)
Highest Point:	72 m (235 ft.)
Lowest Point:	27 m (89 ft.)
Difference in Elevation:	45 m (146 ft.)
Trail Type:	Linear Trail (back and forth)
Is a GPS Device Required?	No
The Nearest Point with Amenities:	The visitors' center has toilets and snacks.

perature drops gradually as the sun is kept away from the narrow gorge. Keep on walking in the Siq until you reach the waterfall. This is the end of the trail. Do not climb down the waterfall. Without ropes, it will be nearly impossible to get back to the visitors' center.

After you have taken in the beauty of the Siq, backtrack down the trail to the visitors' center. When you walk up the steps near the visitors' center, make a right turn over the bridge to check out the hot spring. Most likely, you will see locals camping out here. Be prepared to accept a cup of tea from friendly families before you head back to the car.

Getting There The route to Wadi Bin Hammad is well signposted. Once you are past the little village of Dumna, signs may be difficult to find, however.

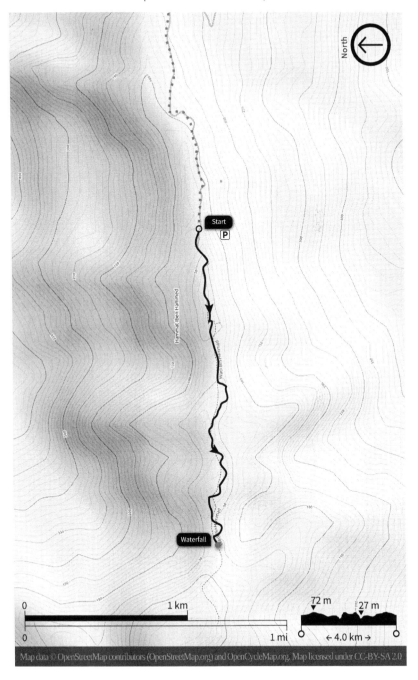

From Amman/Aqaba

Drive south from Amman on Route 15 (the Desert Highway) until you see the turn-off to al-Karak on Route 50, or drive north from Aqaba on Route 15 until you see the turn-off to al-Karak on Route 50.

At the turn-off to al-Karak, drive for 32 km (20 miles) to al-Karak and make a right turn north onto the King's Highway (Route 35) in the direction of Batir (Bateer). After 7 km (4.3 miles) driving north, make a left turn and turn right after 1.1 km (0.7 miles).

Drive for 3.7 km (2.3 miles) and follow the main road to the right. After 1.1 km (0.7 miles), the road curves to the left. Continue driving on the road for 4.4 km (2.7 miles) and turn left. From this point, drive another 1.2 km (0.7 miles) and follow the main road to the left. Follow this road for 7.4 km (4.6 miles) on steep slopes descending into the valley on your right until you reach Wadi Bin Hammad.

Trail Notes

- We recommend that you do not drink water from the wadi.
- Be aware of flash floods in the winter. Please do not hike in the wadi if it rains or has rained 24 hours prior to your planned hike.
- Bring extra socks and shoes that can become wet because you need to walk through shallow water.
- In winter, this can be a cold hike and water levels may be hazardous. Check the weather and be prepared. The park may be closed.
- You can download from our website an E-trail that leads from the King's Highway to the valley. The file is named "11-1 Wadi Bin Hammad Tropical Rain Forest Trail - Directions."
- After the waterfall at the end of the trail, the wadi leads to the Dead Sea at Ghor Haditha (Hadha). You will need ropes or a ladder to navigate the 3 m (9 ft.) waterfall to descend into the wadi if you want to walk 18 km (11.2 miles) to the Dead Sea.
- You can easily combine a visit to Wadi Bin Hammad with a lunch stop at the Karak Castle for a full day of adventure and pleasure.
- If you come from Madaba, you will be driving

over the Mujib Dam as part of the King's Highway (Route 35). This is a spectacular drive, with magnificent views of the Wadi Mujib valley on either side of the dam.

Video Notes

0:21	-	The steep access road to Wadi Bin Hammad. The valley is on your right when you are driving towards Wadi Bin Hammad.
0:28	-	At the entrance where you can buy a ticket.
1:01	-	The public toilets and the "restaurant."
1:05	-	Follow the steps into the wadi.
1:13	-	It is nearly impossible to avoid getting wet feet.
1:24	-	Small waterfall in the wadi.
1:43	-	The Siq leading to the waterfall at the end.
1:50	-	The waterfall at the end. Unless you have ropes or a ladder, this is the end of the trail.

In the Siq of Wadi Bin Hammad

Wadi Ghuweir Trail to Feynan

Introduction

Possibly the most spectacular hike in Jordan, this beautiful but demanding trail guides you through a canyon of tropical foliage as if you were wandering through a "lost world." The Wadi Ghuweir Trail to Feynan is truly a beautiful and quiet hike through a wadi with a 3 km (1.9 miles) Siq and water all the way.

Rarely visited by tourists, there is plenty of vegetation including hanging gardens in the walls of the Siq fed by water seeping from the cliffs. This is an excellent hike to turn into an overnighter. You can camp in the lower parts of Wadi Ghuweir before it widens or you can stay at the Feynan Eco Lodge.

It takes a full day of hiking (8 hours, 15 km, 9.3 miles) to arrive at the Feynan Eco Lodge. If you plan to camp overnight in the wadi, be cognizant of the extra weight of the camping equipment you need to carry in sometimes challenging terrain. A GPS device or guide is recommended.

Trail Description

From where you leave the car, follow the flowing creek downstream in the wadi over smoothed river stones through oleander. Within a few minutes, the wadi narrows into a Siq, and you soon round a bend to find a huge overhang with shade and adorned with tamarix, reeds and oleander. There is a bit of a clamber over boulders here to continue on through lush greenery surrounding the trickling stream. After 1 km (0.6 miles), the cliffs change to yellow domes. The Siq is superb hiking.

In the Siq of Wadi Ghuweir

GPS FILE	12 WADI GHUWEIR TRAIL TO FEYNAN
Duration:	8 hours
Level:	Advanced
Starting Point Coordinates:	N30 35.813 E35 33.984
Starting Point:	At the end of the access road to the wadi.
Is a Four Wheel Drive Car Required?	A 4x4 car is not required. You can park a normal car near the wadi, but we recommend that you arrange a drop-off (see trail notes).
Distance:	15 km (9.3 miles)
Highest Point:	637 m (2,090 ft.)
Lowest Point:	265 m (868 ft.)
Difference in Elevation:	372 m (1,222 ft.)
Trail Type:	Linear Trail (one way)
Is a GPS Device Required?	A GPS device or guide is recommended.
The Nearest Point with Amenities:	No services near the trail until you reach the Feynan Eco Lodge.

Just under 4 km (2.5 miles) from the start is a rock slide (N30 36.008 E35 32.745), easy to get down but difficult to get back up. The Siq continues with a pleasant walk through palms and stepping stones across little ponds full of whirly-gig beetles. There are freshwater crabs here, often in the murkier ponds.

Also keep an eye out for green frogs amongst the reeds. There are plenty of really nice camping places from here down, with plenty of soft sand, running water and shade.

You will come to a small dam. A rough track for 4X4 cars starts here and follows water pipes taking water downstream from the dam. Keep to this track

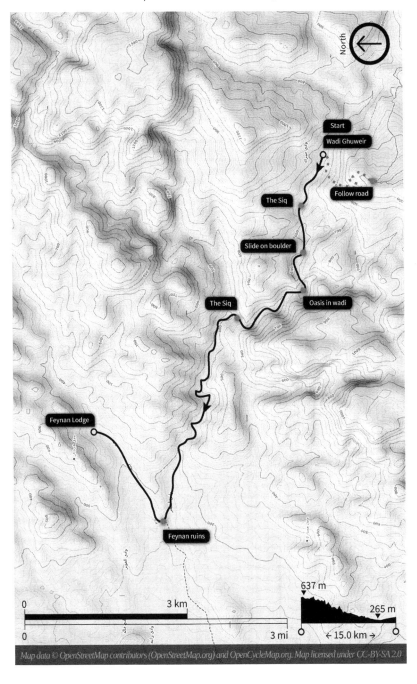

North

Start
Wadi Ghuweir
Follow road
The Siq
Slide on boulder
The Siq
Oasis in wadi
Feynan Lodge
Feynan ruins

637 m

265 m

0

3 km

0

3 mi

← 15.0 km →

for easy walking. Although it is tempting to continue on a more direct course, it doesn't save time or effort.

When the wadi opens, the track intersects with a road. Go east (right) along this road. On the first rise as you exit the riverbed, you will see the sign indicating the Feynan Eco Lodge is ahead.

You pass the Feynan ruins on the right and then have a 3 km (1.9 miles) trudge through some fairly bleak and stony country. You pass through one tiny village consisting of not much more than a school and a few tents, then comes the welcoming sight of the Feynan Eco Lodge.

Getting There

From Amman

Take the Desert Highway (Route 15) south from the 7th Circle in Amman past the airport. After 180 km (112 miles) you reach al-Hushmeyah village. Turn right towards Shobak (ash-Shabak or Shoubak) after 18.2 km (11.3 miles) then turn left on the King's Highway (Route 35). Drive 6.1 km (3.8 miles) until you see the signs to the castle in the village of Shobak.

From Aqaba

From the customs check-point in Aqaba on the Desert Highway (Route 15), drive north for approximately 128 km (79.5 miles) past the city of Ma'an. Turn off the highway via the overpass towards the village of Shobak (ash-Shabak or Shoubak) and drive 18.2 km (11.3 miles) before turning left onto the King's Highway (Route 35) and drive 6.1 km (3.8 miles) until you see the signs to the castle in the village of Shobak.

Continuing from both directions

Whether you come from the direction of Aqaba or Amman, starting from the parking area of the Shobak Castle visitors' center, make a left turn and drive towards the castle. At the T-junction, turn right around the castle into the valley. Follow the curved road for 1.6 km (1 mile) and turn left. Follow this curvy road for another 4.2 km (2.6 miles) passing the town of al-Jayah, until you see a little settlement ahead of you near the town of al-Maqariya (or al-Muqar'iyya) and make a left turn.

After 2.2 km (1.4 miles), turn right before you enter the town of Mansura and again turn right after 150 meters (505 ft.). Make another right turn after 300 meters (0.2 miles). Follow the road for 2.1 km (1.3 miles) and make a left turn to drive up the hillside for 500 meters (0.3 miles). Once you have driven up the hill, the road winds down into the wadi to the left. Park or get dropped off right next to Wadi Ghuweir where there is space for a few cars. If you are leaving your car there overnight, leave a note on the windscreen stating your hiking intentions to avoid instigating a search by Tourist Police.

Tip

See also the trail notes for more information on whether you should keep your car there overnight.

Make sure you use the asphalt road on the left at N30 35.301 E35 33.660 that leads to the start of the trail. If you miss the turn-off, you will have to hike several kilometers/miles extra.

About Feynan

- The ruins at Feynan are not far from the Feynan Eco Lodge, the end point of the trail. Walk from the lodge towards the town of Feynan for 2.1 km (1.3 miles) with the dry river bed on your right. You will find the ruins on your left just before you intersect with a large wadi (Wadi Ghuweir).
- The Feynan Eco Lodge can be closed during Ramadan. Please check the RSCN website for the latest information on opening times.
- You pay the entrance fee to the Dana Reserve at the Feynan Eco Lodge if you continue to walk to Dana village.

- We recommend that you do not drink water from the wadi.
- Be aware of flash floods in the winter. Please do not hike in the wadi if it rains or has rained 24 hours prior to your planned hike.
- The trail is isolated and infrequently visited. Ensure someone knows where you are. Do not attempt to hike alone. It is wise to go with a group.
- In winter, this can be a cold hike and water levels may be hazardous. Check the weather and be prepared.
- Arrange a car drop-off at the beginning of the walk to avoid the alarm being raised when your parked car is noticed to be there after dark. We had well meaning tourist police stay overnight at our car while we were hiking the trail.
- You can combine this trail with the Dana Feynan Trail. To arrange this, we recommend that you park your car in Dana village and stay overnight in a local hotel. Arrange an early drop-off at the starting point of Wadi Ghuweir. After a full day of hiking, camp overnight or stay over at the Feynan Eco Lodge to continue the trail to Dana village a day later to return to your car.
- Bring extra socks in case you need to walk through shallow water.

Trail Notes

If you are retracing your steps up Wadi Ghuweir from the Feynan Eco Lodge, walk along the road from the lodge (south-west) keeping the wadi bed to your right. After 3 km (1.9 miles) you pass a large ruined stone building on your left and then the road drops down into the riverbed of Wadi Ghuweir. Walk along the road and take the first track on your left (heading up the wadi) which is a rough 4X4 car track.

Hiking the Trail from the Feynan Eco Lodge

Follow this track and the water pipes beside it until they both cease at a small dam and continue to follow the wadi.

Just less than 4 km (2.5 miles) from the end of the hiking trail is a rock slide (N30 36.008 E35 32.745) that is awkward to get back up. Ensure that you hike at least with another person for the usual reasons, but especially so here as it is difficult to climb the rock slide alone. Even better, hike the trail with a local guide whose services can be obtained through the Feynan Eco Lodge. A guide is useful not only for arranging transport at the end of the trail, but to also ensure that you can leave the wadi as planned after a long day of hiking. In addition, you are supporting the local economy by providing much needed additional employment.

If you travel independently, you will need to arrange a pick-up at the end of the wadi, or be prepared to walk an extra 2.5 km (1.6 miles) uphill to Mansura and organize something there (which may be difficult, as it is a very small village).

Video Notes

0:20	-	You can combine the trail with a visit to the Shobak Castle which is 14 km (8.7 miles) south of Wadi Ghuweir. Please ensure that you have sufficient time for the hike. It will take 8 hours to reach the Feynan Eco Lodge from the start of the wadi in relatively demanding terrain. We recommend that you start early in the morning to avoid you will be hiking in the dark.
0:56	-	The asphalt road leading to the wadi.
1:00	-	The end of the asphalt road.
1:31	-	The magnificent Siq.
2:32	-	The oasis / tropical forest in the wadi.
2:59	-	The wadi opens up after the Siq.
3:07	-	The Feynan ruins.
3:16	-	The Feynan Eco Lodge.

In the Oasis of Wadi Ghuweir

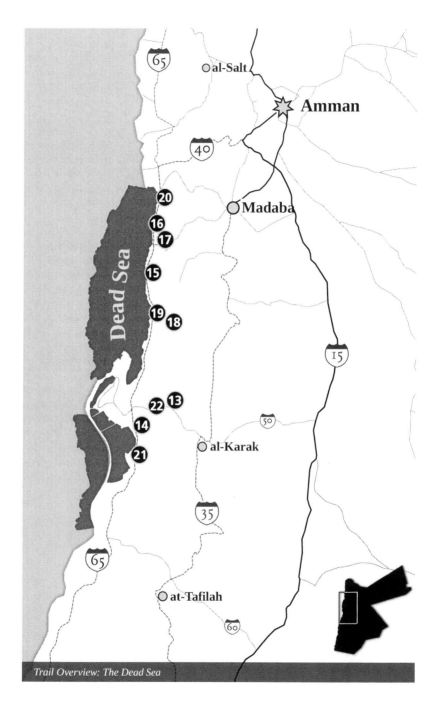

Trail Overview: The Dead Sea

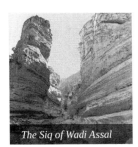

The Siq of Wadi Assal

Region
The Dead Sea

⑬ Wadi Al Karak Waterfalls
⑭ Wadi Assal
⑮ Wadi Attun Hot Springs Trail
⑯ Wadi Himara Palm Trees and Waterfall Trail
⑰ Wadi Himara Panorama Trail
⑱ Wadi Mujib Malaqi Trail
⑲ Wadi Mujib Siq Trail
⑳ Wadi Mukheiris Formation Trail
㉑ Wadi Numeira Siq Trail
㉒ Wadi Weida'a

The Dead Sea
General Notes

Flash Flood in Wadi Mujib

Most trails near the Dead Sea are in narrow wadis (valleys) that are not frequently visited. In general, the following notes apply to the trails described in this section of the guide:

- In summer, this area is very hot with temperatures exceeding 45 °C or 113 °F. Avoid the heat of the day in summer, carry water and use the available shade.
- We recommend that you do not drink water from the wadis.
- In winter, the hikes in the wadis can be cold and water levels may be hazardous. Check the weather and be prepared.
- Since most trails are remote and rarely visited by tourists, it will be unlikely you will encounter Tourist Police if you need assistance.
- We recommend that you leave details of your hike with the owner of your hotel and indicate a time that a search should be instigated.
- You must be self-reliant. Don't expect a passer-by to assist as there are few visitors on most trails.
- Do not attempt to hike alone. It is wise to go with a group.
- Bring extra socks in case you need to walk through shallow water.
- Be aware of flash floods in the winter. Please do not hike in the wadis if it rains or has rained 24 hours prior to your planned hike.

13

The Dead Sea
Wadi Al Karak Waterfalls

Introduction The Wadi Al Karak Waterfalls Trail is in a beautiful valley near the Dead Sea with waterfalls, spectacular cliffs and a fairyland of greenery where the water pours from springs. It follows a sandy river bed and involves frequent wading through a shallow creek. There is plenty of bird life, especially during spring.

Wadi al-Karak affords a leisurely hike with lots of places to stop and enjoy the serenity and the beauty of the place. Since this wadi ends at a small waterfall, there is no danger of getting lost. You do not need a guide or GPS device to enjoy this trail.

Although 12.6 km (7.8 miles) in distance, the wadi is easy to walk with very few areas where you need to navigate through boulders in the riverbed.

Trail Description From the parking area near the water station, head up the (normally dry at this point) creek bed of the wadi, passing oleander, which in spring present a magnificent display of pink flowers. Keep a look out for Tristan's Starling, White Spectacled Bulbuls and Palestinian Sun-birds feeding on the oleander flowers. A bit further tamarix trees appear, and about 600 m (0.4 miles) from the start, you will come upon a creek. Its water is captured and routed for use in the gardens below.

After another glade of oleander, there is a fine old pistachio tree on the left, and more pistachio trees up on the right where the goats can't reach them. As you travel further, you will encounter a nice grove of tamarix.

GPS FILE	13 WADI AL KARAK WATERFALLS
Duration:	5.5 hours
Level:	Easy
Starting Point Coordinates:	N31 16.167 E35 35.188
Starting Point:	At the beginning of the wadi.
Is a Four Wheel Drive Car Required?	A 4x4 car is not required. You can park a normal car near the water station.
Distance:	12.6 km (7.8 miles)
Highest Point:	132 m (433 ft.)
Lowest Point:	-146 m (-478 ft.)
Difference in Elevation:	278 m (911 ft.)
Trail Type:	Linear Trail (back and forth)
Is a GPS Device Required?	No
The Nearest Point with Amenities:	No services near the trail.

Keep following the creek upstream. Spectacular red cliffs close in on both sides and echo the sounds of running water.

After another 3.3 km (2 miles) from the car park, you will find a beautiful waterfall on the left with ferns and palms up the cliff. It is worth a stop here to savor the burbling sound of the water and the greenery after the barren bleakness of Wadi Araba. When you continue, you will immediately encounter a small canyon on the right. Feel free to explore this, but the main trail continues in the canyon to the left, following the stream.

Keep walking until the canyon opens up into an area with two fine waterfalls on the left. This place is a lush fairyland of mist and green, with luxuriant ferns, vines and palms massed over the cliff, while tamarix, oleander, figs and tussock grasses grow at the cliff

Water Irrigation Channels at the Beginning of the Trail

base. This is an excellent place to stop for lunch.

When you have absorbed the scene, continue onwards through the canyon which again narrows to sheer rock walls, smoothed by water flowing over the aeons. After a few minutes, you will come to a massive rock which has crashed down from the heights above and is now firmly wedged in the canyon about 20 m (66 ft.) above the river bed.

Walk under this rock to continue to the end of the trail where the creek releases a waterfall into a shallow gravel pool. This waterfall can only be navigated with ropes.

To return to your car, turn around and follow the stream back down the wadi for 6.3 km (3.9 miles).

Getting There

From Amman

Starting at the 7th Circle in Amman, take Route 40 towards the Dead Sea for 45 km (28 miles) until it merges with the Dead Sea Highway (Route 65). Follow the Dead Sea Highway until you reach the Mujib Bridge and reset your odometer. After 21 km (13 miles) turn left onto an asphalt road and then turn right immediately.

After 0.6 km (0.4 miles) turn left. Drive straight up the hill, passing some houses, and follow the road for 8 km (5 miles). At the end of the road, park the car in front of the little water station.

Do not drive through the town of Ghor Al Mazra'a and do not take Route 50 to Karak when you come from Amman on the Dead Sea Highway. If you come to the turn-off to al-Karak while on the Dead Sea Highway, you have missed the turn-off and driven 3.4 km (2.1 miles) too far south.

From Aqaba

Drive north from Aqaba on the Dead Sea Highway (Route 65) past the settlements of Rahma, Gharandal and Al Safi. After about 2.5 hours (218 km or 135 miles), you pass the turn-off to al-Karak (Route 50)

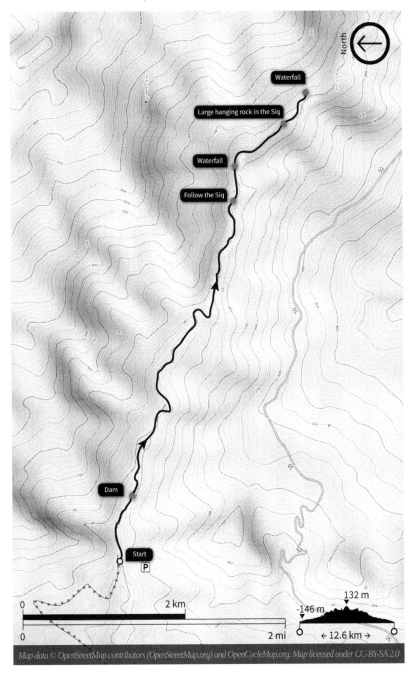

North

Waterfall

Large hanging rock in the Siq

Waterfall

Follow the Siq

Dam

Start
P

0

2 km

0

2 mi

132 m

-146 m

← 12.6 km →

on the right, near Potash City. Continue on the Dead Sea Highway past this turn-off for another 3.4 km (2.1 miles) until you come to a road on the right. Turn onto this road, and turn right again immediately.

After 0.6 km (0.4 miles) turn left. Drive straight up the hill, passing some houses, and follow the road for 8 km (5 miles) to the end of the road and park the car in front of the little water station.

From al-Karak

If you come down on Route 50 from al-Karak, turn right when you reach the Dead Sea Highway to head north in the direction of Amman. After 3.4 km (2.1 miles), take the road on your right and turn right again immediately.

After 0.6 km (0.4 miles) turn left. Drive straight up the hill, passing some houses, and follow the road for 8 km (5 miles). At the end of the road, park the car in front of the little water station.

Trail Notes

- When you drive uphill after leaving the Dead Sea Highway turn-off, you will have a panoramic view of the Dead Sea on the left. You will see an irrigation pipe along the winding road which will lead to the water station near the starting point of the Wadi Al Karak Waterfalls Trail.
- At the beginning of the hike there is little shade to be had. Once you are in the wadi past the dam, there is shade and lots of water to cool off in.
- You can download from *www.hiking-in-jordan.com* an E-trail that leads from the Dead Sea Highway turn-off to the beginning of the trail. The file is named "13-1 Wadi Al Karak Access Road."

Video Notes

0:14 - The road to the trail. You will see irrigation pipes along the road.
0:17 - Starting point of the trail.
0:30 - The dam.
1:44 - The large waterfall.
2:44 - The massive rock which has crashed down from the heights above.
2:53 - The waterfall with the shallow pool at the end of the trail.

The Large Waterfall in Wadi Al Karak

Wadi Assal

14

Wadi Assal provides a full day of hiking with waterfalls, unspoiled nature, diverse wildlife and a beautiful narrow canyon (Siq) near the Dead Sea. Wadi Assal is as diverse a wadi can be with an abundance of oleander, tamarix and acacia near the wadi's stream with the occasional freshwater crab and hidden springs.

Introduction

The trail is moderately difficult, because you need to climb boulders and small rock formations near waterfalls to complete the trail. The hiking video gives you an idea of what to expect. Neither a guide nor a GPS device is required to enjoy the wadi.

At the end of the gravel road, walk into the wadi. You pass an old concrete dam after approximately 650 m (0.4 miles), long since filled by the relentless deposit of sediment washed down by floods. Following the creek up, you will pass an impressive and photogenic column on the right. Continue through oleander and tamarix, and keep an eye out for freshwater crabs in the pools and on the rocks. There are also particularly fine red cliffs on the right further along the trail.

Trail Description

Look for the caper vines hanging down, which adds a touch of blue-green to the scene. Further on, you enter a Siq with a few palms. The Siq starts approximately 2.2 km (1.4 miles) after the dam. You cannot avoid getting wet feet if the creek is flowing. Note the multi-colored sandstones of red, purple and yellow hues.

GPS FILE	14 WADI ASSAL
Duration:	5 hours
Level:	Moderate
Starting Point Coordinates:	N31 11.693 E35 32.522
Starting Point:	At the beginning of the wadi.
Is a Four Wheel Drive Car Required?	A 4x4 car is not required. You can park a normal car on a gravel road near the wadi.
Distance:	11.3 km (7.0 miles)
Highest Point:	-101 m (-332 ft.)
Lowest Point:	-328 m (-1,075 ft.)
Difference in Elevation:	227 m (743 ft.)
Trail Type:	Linear Trail (back and forth)
Is a GPS Device Required?	No
The Nearest Point with Amenities:	No services near the trail.

Follow the wadi and you will come to where the creek jets down a rock chute into the gravel stream bed. The Siq now begins to widen and there is more vegetation with tamarix and oleander. There are some interesting tiered rock formations and just a few paces on is a spring issuing from the rock on the left. This is underground water pouring out in a clear and enticing stream, in contrast to the sediment-filled water coming down the wadi.

Follow the wadi and you will come to a very pleasant spot with a waterfall and a dripping overhang with maidenhair ferns. Keep an eye out for crabs crawling the rocks, either on the rock ledges or on the moss and algae.

From here on, the vegetation gets thicker with lots of cane with the tamarix and oleander making it harder to walk. There is a place suitable as a campsite at 5

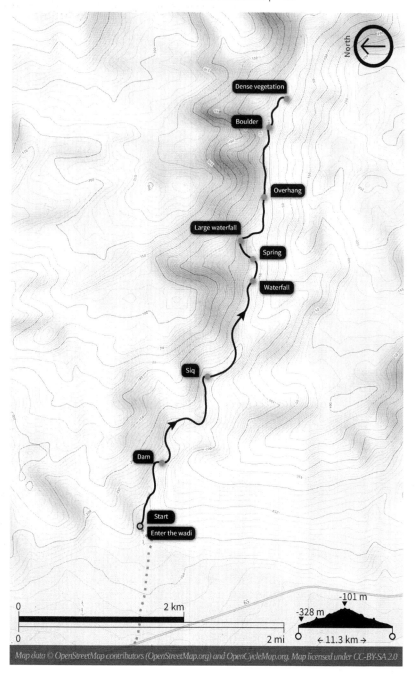

km (3.1 miles) from the dam. You could keep walking if you manage to navigate through the dense vegetation at the end of the trail, but you are past the most interesting part of the wadi. From here, retrace your steps to the car.

Getting There   *From Amman*

Starting at the 7th Circle in Amman, take Route 40 towards the Dead Sea for 45 km (28 miles) until it merges with the Dead Sea Highway (Route 65). Follow the Dead Sea Highway until you reach the Mujib Bridge and reset your odometer.

Approximately 31 km (19.3 miles) south of the Wadi Mujib Bridge, look for a gravel road on the left. Follow the gravel road up the middle of a stony wadi. There may be a few Bedouin tents here. Feel free to give the locals a wave and exchange pleasantries.

Continue on to cross a stream several times before driving up in it. It is gravel and not likely to bog you, but drive with care and beware of boulders. Drive into the wadi with oleander, tamarix and acacia and find a parking spot.

From Aqaba

Drive north from Aqaba on the Dead Sea Highway (Route 65) for about 2 hours. While driving north, you will pass the settlements of Rahma, Gharandal and Al Safi. You will pass the sign for "Lut's Cave" when the road curves to the left. Set you odometer and look for a gravel road on the right after 15.8 km (9.9 miles). You will pass the smokestacks of the Arab Potash Company in Potash City and the Bromine Factory (both on the left side of the road). The gravel road you want leads east (to the right) up the middle of a stony wadi.

If you come to the Karak turn-off to Route 50 you have come too far. Turn around and drive back 6.4 km (4 miles) and turn left onto the gravel road.

Drive up the gravel road crossing a stream several times before driving up in it. It is gravel and not likely to bog you down, but beware of boulders. Drive into the wadi for a parking spot. Continue walking towards the dam.

Trail Notes

- With a 2WD drive, it may not be always suitable to drive into the wadi. Park your car near the gravel road and start walking into the wadi, away from the Dead Sea.
- You can download from our website an E-trail that leads from the Dead Sea Highway to the beginning of the trail on the gravel road. The file is named "14-1 Wadi Assal Access Road."
- You can see the clear and enticing stream, in contrast to the sediment-filled water coming down the wadi in one of the "off the record" videos on the YouTube Channel and the Hiking in Jordan website. The video is called: "Nice Clean and Delicious Water, Chris?" To be exact, the spring in the video can be found at N31 11.065 E35 34.082.

Video Notes

0:21	-	You may see Bedouin tents near the gravel road.
0:22	-	The gravel road from the Dead Sea Highway that leads to the wadi.
0:24	-	You may want to park a normal 2WD car in this area. We parked our 4X4 car in the wadi (0:50).
1:09	-	The dam.
1:31	-	The Siq.
2:09	-	You need to be able to navigate small rock formations near the waterfalls and boulders to reach the end of the trail.
2:26	-	Underground water is issuing out in a stream.

The Siq in the Wadi

The Dead Sea
Wadi Attun
Hot Springs Trail

Trail
15

This relatively demanding trail leads to natural hot springs, palm trees and waterfalls in a relatively unknown wadi near the Dead Sea. The wadi is surrounded by high cliffs of red stone and has an abundance of ferns and other vegetation.

Introduction

Because the trail is rarely visited, you most likely will be wandering by yourself in this unexpectedly clean, untouched wadi. You could almost forget that you are in the middle of the desert near the lowest point on earth.

Near the Dead Sea

Although short in distance (2.3 km, 1.4 miles), you need to be able to navigate boulders in the wadi to reach the waterfall at the end of the trail. A GPS device or guide is not required, as you cannot get lost in the wadi.

Trail Description   After you have parked the car near the bridge crossing the wadi, descend into the river bed and follow the small river upstream leaving the Dead Sea behind. You will see interesting formations of palm trees near the wadi after 600 m (0.4 miles). Within a few minutes of the palm trees, you reach the hot springs. It is a great experience to sit in a natural hot spring if you do not mind the heat. The area near the hot springs is also ideal for camping if you like to stay overnight.

The trail continues on the right side of the rock formation near the hot springs. Climb the hillside with the springs to your left until you reach the top of the hill. At this point, turn around for magnificent views of the Dead Sea. Follow the wadi until you reach the waterfall at the end of the trail.

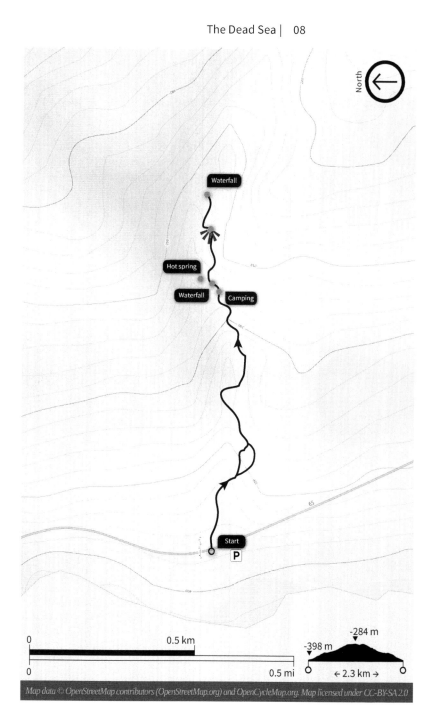

GPS FILE	15 WADI ATTUN HOT SPRINGS TRAIL
Duration:	2.5 hours
Level:	Moderate
Starting Point Coordinates:	N31 32.726 E35 33.402
Starting Point:	At the beginning of the wadi.
Is a Four Wheel Drive Car Required?	A 4x4 car is not required. You can park a normal car near the Dead Sea Highway.
Distance:	2.3 km (1.4 miles)
Highest Point:	-284 m (-932 ft.)
Lowest Point:	-398 m (-1,307 ft.)
Difference in Elevation:	114 m (375 ft.)
Trail Type:	Linear Trail (back and forth)
Is a GPS Device Required?	No
The Nearest Point with Amenities:	No services near the trail.

Getting There   *From Amman*

Starting at the 7th Circle in Amman, take Route 40 towards the Dead Sea for 45 km (28 miles) until it merges with the Dead Sea Highway (Route 65). From the hotel area, continue to drive south and pass (but do not take) the Panoramic Complex turn-off on your left. From this turn-off drive for another 12.4 km (7.7 miles) on Route 65 passing Wadi Zarqa Ma'in. Park on the left of the road in a small parking area just before the bridge that crosses the wadi.

If you have reached the Mujib Bridge, you have driven too far south. From the bridge, turn around and drive back north for 9 km (5.6 miles) on the Dead Sea Highway until you cross the bridge over the wadi and park on the right side of the road.

From Aqaba

Drive north from Aqaba on the Dead Sea Highway (Route 65) for about 3 hours or 224 km (139 miles) from the Aqaba customs check-point until you reach the Mujib Bridge. While driving north, you will pass the settlements of Rahma, Gharandal, Al Safi and Potash City. Cross the Mujib Bridge and drive for another 9 km (5.6 miles) until you cross the bridge over the wadi and park on the right side of the road.

Trail Notes

The springs can be really hot. We recommend against jumping in before testing their temperature.

Video Notes

0:14	-	The bridge crossing the wadi near the beginning of the trail.
0:21	-	You will see palm trees near the start of the trail.
1:03	-	Your feet will get wet.
1:38	-	The natural hot spring in the wadi.
1:42	-	The hot spring seen from the top of the hill. The trail continues on the right side of the rock formation near the hot spring.
2:23	-	The waterfall at the end of the trail.

16 Wadi Himara Palm Trees and Waterfall Trail

Introduction This is a short wadi with red cliffs and a scree slope with juniper, oleander, reeds, capers and palms. You will rock hop along a stream with small waterfalls and pools. A GPS device or guide is not required as you will be wandering through the wadi that ends near a small waterfall.

Trail Description Clamber down from the bridge at the Dead Sea Highway to the creek bed to begin the walk along the boulders up the wadi. Follow the small, and at the beginning rather uninviting, creek through scattered tamarix.

You will quickly find the place much more inviting once amongst the capers, juniper and palms. Walk upstream following the brook between red cliffs and scree-slopes to encounter oleander, small waterfalls and little pools surrounded by reeds.

Stay to the right and continue up the main Siq. You will find yourself climbing over boulders and between red mudstone cliffs. The walk rises in steps with a series of tiny waterfalls and palms, capers and pampas up the cliffs. It ends at an impassable 4 m (13 ft.) waterfall. Return downstream to arrive back at the bridge after 1.7 km (1.1 miles), where you have parked the car.

About Junipers Junipers are coniferous trees in the genus *Juniperus* which are in the cypress family *Cupressaceae*. There are around 60 species distributed throughout the northern hemisphere. A juniper "berry" is actually

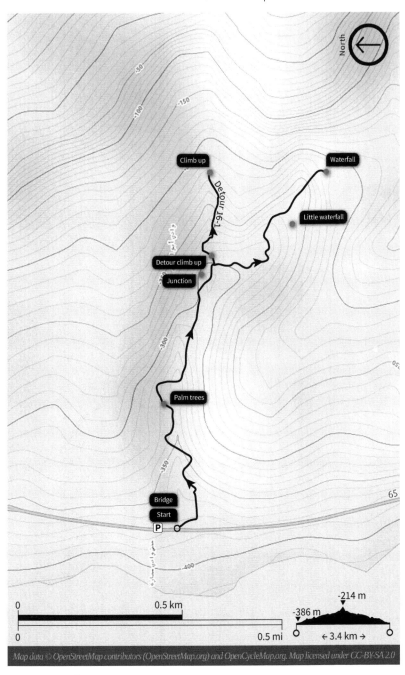

GPS FILE	16 WADI HIMARA PALM TREES AND WATERFALL TRAIL
Duration:	2 hours
Level:	Moderate
Starting Point Coordinates:	N31 38.788 E35 34.457
Starting Point:	At the beginning of the wadi.
Is a Four Wheel Drive Car Required?	A 4x4 car is not required. You can park a normal car near the Dead Sea Highway.
Distance:	3.4 km (2.1 miles)
Highest Point:	-214 m (-702 ft.)
Lowest Point:	-386 m (-1,267 ft.)
Difference in Elevation:	172 m (565 ft.)
Trail Type:	Linear Trail (back and forth)
Is a GPS Device Required?	No
The Nearest Point with Amenities:	The Dead Sea Panoramic Complex and the hotels area at the Dead Sea.

a female seed cone with fleshy and merged scales. The cones from a handful of species, especially *Juniperus communis*, are used as a spice, particularly in European cuisine, and also give gin its distinctive flavor.

Getting There   *From Amman*
Starting at the 7th Circle in Amman, take Route 40 towards the Dead Sea for 45 km (28 miles) until it merges with the Dead Sea Highway (Route 65). Continue to drive south to the Panoramic Complex turn-off that is on your left. Ignore the turn-off and cross a small bridge over Wadi Himara 800 m (0.5 miles) past the Panoramic Complex turn-off. Park your car in the gravel area by the bridge on the right side of the road.

From Madaba

Drive to the town of Ma'in and follow the road to-wards the Dead Sea. Ignore the turn-off on the left to the Ma'in Hot Springs and continue driving to the Panoramic Complex. After you have passed the Panoramic Complex situated on the left side of the road, continue driving to the Dead Sea. Turn left on the Dead Sea Highway (Route 65) and cross a small bridge over Wadi Himara 800 m (0.5 miles) past the Panoramic Complex turn-off. Park your car in the gravel area by the bridge on the right side of the road.

From Aqaba

Drive north from Aqaba on the Dead Sea Highway (Route 65). While driving north, you will pass the settlements of Rahma, Gharandal, Al Safi and Potash City. From the Mujib Bridge, continue to drive 21 km (13 miles) until you come to a small bridge. Pull over just before the bridge and park on the left side of the road. The parking area is 800 m (0.5 miles) south of the Panoramic Complex turn-off on the Dead Sea Highway.

Trail Notes

Although the Wadi Himara Palm Trees and Waterfall Trail is located in the area of the Wadi Himara Panorama Trail, the two trails are not connected with a hiking path. You need to climb and use ropes to connect the two trails.

Extended / Alternative Version

Wadi Himara Palm Trees and Waterfall Trail with Detour

After 800 m (0.5 miles) from the start of the trail, the canyon continues to the right. At this point, you can make a detour by climbing up on the left for about 5 m (20 ft.) into a Siq. The narrowness of this Siq makes it dangerous if a lot of water is coming down, so do not proceed if there is any chance of rain upstream.

There are more capers along the cliffs as you continue along the Siq that comes to a dead end with a set of natural stairs. These are fun to climb (with care) but they lead nowhere and you will have to turn back and head down to meet the main Siq again.

Wildlife in the Wadi

GPS FILE	16-1 WADI HIMARA PALM TREES AND WATERFALL TRAIL WITH DETOUR
Duration:	2.5 hours
Level:	Moderate
Starting Point Coordinates:	N31 38.788 E35 34.457
Starting Point:	At the beginning of the wadi.
Is a Four Wheel Drive Car Required?	A 4x4 car is not required. You can park a normal car near the Dead Sea Highway.
Distance:	4.0 km (2.5 miles)
Highest Point:	-221 m (-725 ft.)
Lowest Point:	-386 m (-1,267 ft.)
Difference in Elevation:	165 m (542 ft.)
Trail Type:	Linear Trail (back and forth)
Is a GPS Device Required?	No
The Nearest Point with Amenities:	The Dead Sea Panoramic Complex and the hotels area at the Dead Sea.

Video Notes

0:28 - The parking area near the bridge on the Dead Sea Highway. The parking area is on the left side before the bridge if you come from the direction of Aqaba. The parking area is on the right side after you have crossed the bridge if you come from the direction of Amman.

0:37 - Enter the wadi on the right side after you have walked over the bridge from the direction of Aqaba.

2:13 - Chris and Greg are climbing up to a step at the beginning of the detour trail.

2:23 - The natural stairs (on the detour trail).

2:58 - The waterfall at the end of the trail.

The Dead Sea

17

Wadi Himara Panorama Trail

Introduction This is a short wadi walk with juniper, oleander, tamarix, caper and palms plus an incredible view at the end. It is a great place to have a picnic and absorb one of the best views of the Dead Sea from a beautiful and infrequently visited location. If you are lucky, you will meet local Bedouins enjoying a cup of tea in the wadi. A GPS device or guide is not required, although you need to be able to find your way on the steep slope into the wadi. You cannot get lost in the wadi.

You can combine the trail with a visit to the nearby Panoramic Complex for lunch and excellent views.

Trail Description From the bridge, head down the wadi through oleander, juniper and tamarix with capers draping from the cliffs. Follow the creek as it tumbles down boulders of conglomerate and limestone. When you come to a waterfall, leave the creek and keep to the left, staying high to pick your way along the left slope. Don't be tempted to descend yet or you will be punished for your audacity.

After 804 m (0.5 miles) from the bridge, descend to the creek after you pass a second waterfall. You will need to take special care when choosing a path down the slope, as it is steep with loose material. Take time to find stable ground.

Once back at the creek, palms and other vegetation create a pleasant scene. Follow the creek from here down to the end of the trail with exceptionally fine

GPS File	17 Wadi Himara Panorama Trail
Duration:	2 hours
Level:	Moderate
Starting Point Coordinates:	N31 38.322 E35 36.082
Starting Point:	Near the bridge.
Is a Four Wheel Drive Car Required?	A 4x4 car is not required. You can park a normal car near the bridge.
Distance:	2.7 km (1.7 miles)
Highest Point:	159 m (521 ft.)
Lowest Point:	-36 m (-119 ft.)
Difference in Elevation:	195 m (640 ft.)
Trail Type:	Linear Trail (back and forth)
Is a GPS Device Required?	No
The Nearest Point with Amenities:	The Dead Sea Panoramic Complex and the hotels area at the Dead Sea.

views. You will find yourself gazing over the vastness of the Dead Sea from the top of the highest waterfall in Jordan. It really is extraordinary when you realize that at this majestic height over this truly huge valley, you are standing only 36 m (119 ft.) below sea level. Enjoy the view before heading back to the car the same way you came.

Getting There

From Amman

Starting at the 7th Circle in Amman, take Route 40 towards the Dead Sea for 45 km (28 miles) until it merges with the Dead Sea Highway (Route 65). Continue to drive south to the Panoramic Complex turn-off.

Make a left turn onto the road and head uphill towards the Panoramic Complex. You will cross the Wadi Abu Al-Asal bridge and then a second bridge across Wadi Himara. This is the last bridge before the

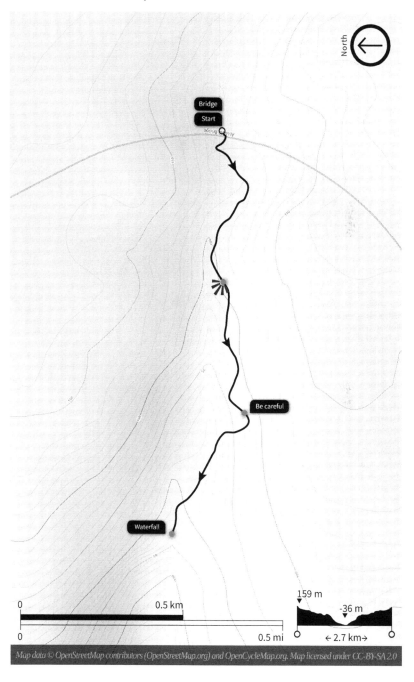

North

Bridge
Start

Be careful

Waterfall

0   0.5 km

0   0.5 mi

159 m
-36 m
← 2.7 km →

Panoramic Complex. The trail starts at this bridge. If you have driven to the entrance of the Panoramic Complex, you have gone too far. Turn around and drive until you see the bridge and park your car.

From Madaba

Drive to the town of Ma'in and keep on following the road towards the Dead Sea. Ignore the turn-off on the left side to the Ma'in Hot Springs and continue driving to the Panoramic Complex. After you have passed the Panoramic Complex situated on the left side of the road, park your car after 1.6 km (1 mile) before you cross the first bridge after the Panoramic Complex.

From Aqaba

Drive north from Aqaba on the Dead Sea Highway (Route 65) and pass the settlements of Rahma, Gharandal, Al Safi and Potash City. From the Mujib Bridge, drive 21 km (13.4 miles) north and make a right turn onto the road towards the Panoramic Complex. You will cross the Wadi Abu Al-Asal bridge and then a second bridge across Wadi Himara. This is the last bridge before the Panoramic Complex. The trail starts at this bridge. If you have driven to the entrance of the Panoramic Complex, you have gone too far. Turn around and drive until you see the bridge and park your car.

At the time of writing, immediately after the Wadi Himara bridge coming from the Dead Sea (the second bridge), there was a gap in the guard rail on the left with a 2WD track you can take down to the base of the bridge. Park here. Failing that, park somewhere safe near the bridge and walk down to where the trail starts at the base of the bridge.

Trail Notes

- Although you are on top of Jordan's tallest waterfall at the end of the trail, you will not see much of the waterfall.
- The drop-off at the end of the trail is very steep and we strongly recommend that you refrain from exploring the waterfall beyond the end point of the trail. Do not climb on the rock formation to the right at the end of the trail.
- At the Panoramic Complex, the RSCN has developed an exhibition along the cliff called the "Zara Cliff Trail." It is an easy self-guided walk (1.4 km, 0.7 miles round trip) with several vistas with exhibits highlighting unique aspects of the area.

Interesting Architectural Design of the Panoramic Complex

0:13	-	The turn-off to the Panoramic Complex from the Dead Sea Highway leads to the town of Madaba, the Ma'in Hot Springs and Mount Nebo.
0:27	-	This is the bridge across Wadi Himara and the last bridge that you will cross when you come from the Dead Sea Highway. Please note that the video of the bridge is taken from a distance. At 0:40 you can see where we parked the car under the bridge using the gap in the guard rail.
0:29	-	The 2WD track that you can take to the base of the bridge as long as the guard rail has not been repaired. Otherwise, you will need to park your car near the road.
1:47	-	There are small waterfalls along the trail.
2:03	-	A spectacular view of the Dead Sea on top of Jordan's tallest waterfall at the end of the trail.
2:09	-	The Dead Sea Panoramic Complex near the trail is a great place for lunch and cold drinks.

Video Notes

The Dead Sea

18

Wadi Mujib Malaqi Trail

Introduction
This trail leads from the Mujib Bridge near the Dead Sea to the famous Wadi al-Mujib valley in the Mujib Biosphere Reserve, the lowest reserve on earth. UNESCO formally recognized the Mujib Nature Reserve as a Biosphere Reserve in 2011.

This is not a self-guided tour. You need climbing equipment to rappel a 30 m (98 ft.) waterfall and you can enter the reserve only with a guide as part of a group. The climbing equipment, life jacket and guides are provided by the Royal Society for the Conservation of Nature (RSCN).

You need to be at least 18 years old and capable of swimming to enter the reserve. We recommend that you make reservations prior to arriving at the reserve. A GPS device is not required.

Trail Description
From the Mujib Biosphere Reserve visitors' center, a Jeep will bring you to the beginning of the trail. After the drop-off point, 2 km (1.2 miles) from the visitors' center, you will be walking uphill towards the wadi with nice views of the Dead Sea and its surroundings. After 2.4 km (1.5 miles), you reach the wadi. Follow the wadi upstream, occasionally zigzagging through dense vegetation, for 1.1 km (0.7 miles) to reach a nice picnic area. From this point, you can swim further upstream in the warm water of the wadi until you reach a rock formation in the water at a dead end.

GPS FILE	18 WADI MUJIB MALAQI TRAIL
Duration:	4.5 hours
Level:	Moderate
Starting Point Coordinates:	N31 28.035 E35 34.381
Starting Point:	Mujib Reserve visitors' center.
Is a Four Wheel Drive Car Required?	A 4x4 car is not required. You can park a normal car at the visitors' center.
Distance:	6.9 km (4.3 miles)[1]
Highest Point:	-188 m (-618 ft.)
Lowest Point:	-412 m (-1,352 ft.)
Difference in Elevation:	224 m (734 ft.)
Trail Type:	Circular Trail
Is a GPS Device Required?	No, since a guide is mandatory.
The Nearest Point with Amenities:	The visitors' center has toilets.

Head back to the picnic area to walk and swim downstream in the wadi for 2.4 km (1.5 miles) until you reach the large waterfall. Rappel the 30 m (98 ft.) waterfall with the equipment provided by your guide. You need this equipment to reach the lower part of the wadi under the watchful eyes of spectators in colorful life jackets who have been walking the Wadi Mujib Siq Trail *(» page 162)* that ends at this waterfall. From this point, it is 900 m (0.6 miles) to the visitors' center.

From Amman **Getting There**

The Mujib Biosphere Reserve is near the Mujib Bridge on the Dead Sea Highway (Route 65). Starting at the 7th Circle in Amman, take Route 40 towards the Dead Sea for 45 km (28 miles) until it merges with the Dead Sea Highway (Route 65). Follow the Dead Sea Highway until you reach the Mujib Bridge. The

1   The distance of the Jeep ride is not included.

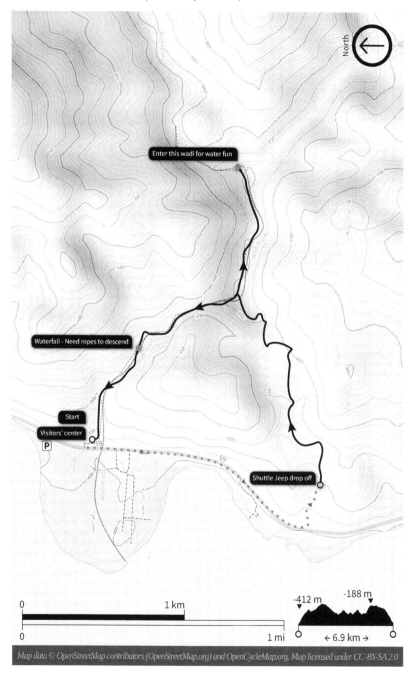

North

Enter this wadi for water fun

Waterfall - Need ropes to descend

Start

Visitors' center

P

Shuttle Jeep drop off

| 0 | | 1 km |
| 0 | | 1 mi |

-412 m   -188 m
← 6.9 km →

A View from the Top of the Waterfall

Mujib Biosphere Reserve visitors' center is on your left before you cross the bridge.

Although the RSCN calculates 1.5 hours to get to Mujib from Amman, we recommend you reserve 2.5 hours to travel by car to ensure you have extra time to navigate traffic in Amman and enjoy the Dead Sea area before you hike.

From Aqaba

Drive north from the Aqaba customs check-point on the Dead Sea Highway (Route 65) for about 3.5 hours or 224 km (139 miles) until you reach the Mujib Bridge. While driving north, you will pass the settlements of Rahma, Gharandal, Al Safi and Potash City. Cross the Mujib Bridge and park the car on your right near the visitors' center.

Trail Notes

- Because of the threat of flash floods and general high water levels, the Wadi Mujib Malaqi Trail is open only between April 1 and October 31.
- Bring extra socks, shoes and clothing because you need to walk and occasionally swim in shallow water.
- We also recommend you bring a waterproof camera or a watertight bag to protect your camera.
- Please note the age restriction imposed by the RSCN. Visitors must be at least 18 years to enter the reserve, even on "dry trails."
- The RSCN also requires that you can swim and that you have a reasonable level of fitness and no fear of heights in order to rappel the waterfall.
- Hanging in ropes navigating the waterfall can be a bit daunting at first when you put on the harness, but you will get used to it quickly. A guide is waiting below the waterfall to assist you while you go down. Day visitors on the Wadi Mujib Siq Trail will be applauding your endeavor.
- The guided group normally leaves at 8 AM. Check the RSCN website for times.

Video Notes

0:12 - The Wadi Mujib Bridge near the visitors' center.

0:22 - A short Jeep ride will bring you to the beginning of the trail.

0:32 - Drop-off point near the wadi.

1:17 - The beginning of the wadi. You will absolutely get wet.

2:05 - Start of the narrow canyon.

2:38 - The large waterfall near the end of the trail.

You Need Ropes to Descend

Wadi Mujib Siq Trail

Introduction

The Wadi Mujib Siq Trail is a nice option to spend pleasant time in warm fresh water near the Dead Sea during the hot summers in Jordan. You will be mostly spending time swimming and bathing while you are surrounded by boulders and fast-moving water streams. Be prepared to climb up slippery boulders with the assistance of short ropes attached to the boulders to get to the endpoint of the trail. You do not need a GPS device, climbing equipment or a guide to complete this short trail. You cannot make reservations. Entrance to the wadi is determined by a first-come, first served, basis until they run out of 80 life jackets.

Trail Description

From the visitors' center, grab your life jacket after you have paid your entrance fee and walk on the bridge that hugs the cliff into the wadi. From this point, start walking upstream. While you work your way up, you will encounter boulders that you can navigate with short ropes that are firmly attached to the rock formations above the water line. Once you have navigated the slippery boulders, you will see the large waterfall at the endpoint of the trail.

You may see people rappel the waterfall who have been hiking the Wadi Mujib Malaqi Trail (» page 155). The best chance to see people descend the waterfall is normally around 12:30 PM.

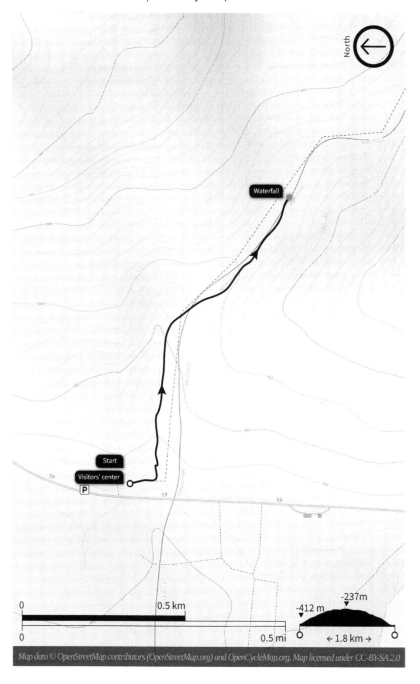

Starting Point of the Trail

GPS FILE	19 WADI MUJIB SIQ TRAIL
Duration:	2.5 hours
Level:	Easy
Starting Point Coordinates:	N31 28.035 E35 34.381
Starting Point:	Mujib Reserve visitors' center.
Is a Four Wheel Drive Car Required?	A 4x4 car is not required. You can park a normal car at the visitors' center.
Distance:	1.8 km (1.1 miles)
Highest Point:	-237 m (-778 ft.)
Lowest Point:	-412 m (-1,352 ft.)
Difference in Elevation:	175 m (574 ft.)
Trail Type:	Linear Trail (back and forth)
Is a GPS Device Required?	No
The Nearest Point with Amenities:	The visitors' center has toilets.

Notes, Getting There   See Wadi Mujib Malaqi Trail *(» page 155).*

Video Notes

0:12	-	The parking area near the Mujib Biosphere Reserve visitors' center.
0:19	-	You enter the wadi from the visitors' center using the metal stairs.
0:55	-	The Siq in the wadi.
0:59	-	You absolutely will get wet.
1:04	-	The waterfall at the end of the trail (seen from the top).

Wadi Mukheiris Formation Trail

Introduction

Located in the middle of the Dead Sea hotel area, this wonderful wadi is not far from Amman and can be navigated relatively easily, although you need to be able to navigate the boulders in the wadi. You will be rewarded with palm trees, water cascades, freshwater crabs and lush vegetation in this surprisingly beautiful wadi, despite the rather intimidating flash flood defense system in the beginning of the wadi.

You do not need a guide or GPS device to stay on the trail, which leads to a large boulder with a small waterfall and clear water pool.

Trail Description

Enter the access road north of the bridge and follow the road and later a path for 320 m (0.2 miles). Find your way down on a steep slope into the wadi. This is probably one of the more difficult things to do on this trail. Do not climb over the defense system.

Within 75 m (246 ft.), you will see a second flood defense system with water breakers. Find your way through the breakers on the left and walk towards the waterfall for 550 m (0.3 miles), which you can bypass on the right side of the wadi. After 300 m (0.2 miles), the wadi starts to narrow with boulders in the riverbed. Within another 300 m (0.2 miles), you will see a large boulder in the wadi. You can climb under the boulder and continue walking east in the wadi while you enjoy the surroundings with palm trees, lush vegetation and the occasional freshwater crab resting on the wet rock formations near the stream.

GPS File	20 Wadi Mukheiris Formation Trail
Duration:	3.5 hours
Level:	Moderate
Starting Point Coordinates:	N31 43.236 E35 35.458
Starting Point:	At the beginning of the wadi.
Is a Four Wheel Drive Car Required?	A 4x4 car is not required. You can park a normal car near the Dead Sea Highway.
Distance:	5.8 km (3.6 miles)
Highest Point:	-203 m (-665 ft.)
Lowest Point:	-356 m (-1,168 ft.)
Difference in Elevation:	153 m (503 ft.)
Trail Type:	Linear Trail (back and forth)
Is a GPS Device Required?	No
The Nearest Point with Amenities:	Dead Sea hotels.

The trail ends at the large boulder near the water pool and the small waterfall. From this point, it is 2.9 km (1.8 miles) back to the car. You can continue to explore the wadi if you are willing to get really wet. A rope was attached to the boulder to climb up when this was written.

Getting There *From Amman*
Starting at the 7th Circle in Amman, take Route 40 towards the Dead Sea for 45 km (28 miles) until it merges with the Dead Sea Highway (Route 65). Follow the Dead Sea Highway for 9.7 km (6 miles) until you are near the convention center and in the hotel area. You will see the large flash flood defense system in the wadi on your left with the Dead Sea on your right.

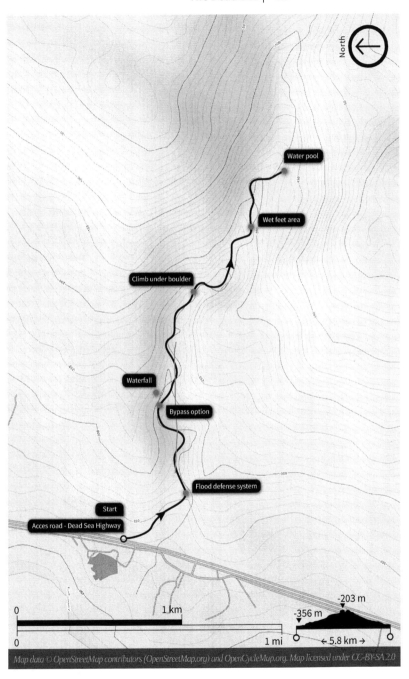

North

Water pool

Wet feet area

Climb under boulder

Waterfall

Bypass option

Flood defense system

Start

Acces road - Dead Sea Highway

0   1 km

0   1 mi

-203 m

-356 m

← 5.8 km →

From Aqaba

Drive north from Aqaba on the Dead Sea Highway (Route 65) for about 3 hours or 224 km (139 miles) from the Aqaba customs check-point until you reach the Mujib Bridge. While driving north, you will pass the settlements of Rahma, Gharandal, Al Safi and Potash City. Cross the Mujib Bridge and drive for another 21 km (13.4 miles) north until the Panoramic Complex turn-off and reset your odometer.

Stay on the Dead Sea Highway and drive 7.8 km (4.9 miles). You will see the large flash flood defense system in the wadi on your right with the Dead Sea and the convention center on your left.

Trail Notes
- You can park your car near the hotels in the area.
- The flash flood defense system in the beginning of the wadi is rather intimidating. We recommend that you do not climb over the system, but that you descend into the wadi on a steep slope at the end of the system when you are 75 m (246 ft.) from the water breakers (made of pillars) in the wadi.

About the Mukheiris Formation
- The Mukheiris Formation was named after Wadi Mukheiris by Klaus Bandel and Hani Khoury in 1981.
- The formation consists of calcareous sandstone intercalated with sand and clay and dates back to the early Ladinian stage, 235 million years ago.
- In 1975, Bandel and his team found a well pre-served mandible (lower jaw) of a four-limbed vertebrate (tetrapod) during geological fieldwork east of the trail. It belonged to a "stereospondyl amphibian," an early species that walked on land.

Video Notes

0:25	-	The flash flood defense system at the beginning of the wadi.
0:36	-	The second flood defense system with the water breakers (made of pillars).
1:04	-	The wadi at the start of the trail. It narrows as you progress with the hike.
1:10	-	Water cascades in the wadi.
1:45	-	You need to be able to navigate boulders to complete the trail.
2:14	-	The trail ends at the large boulder with the small waterfall and water pool.

Flood Defense System at the Beginning of the Trail

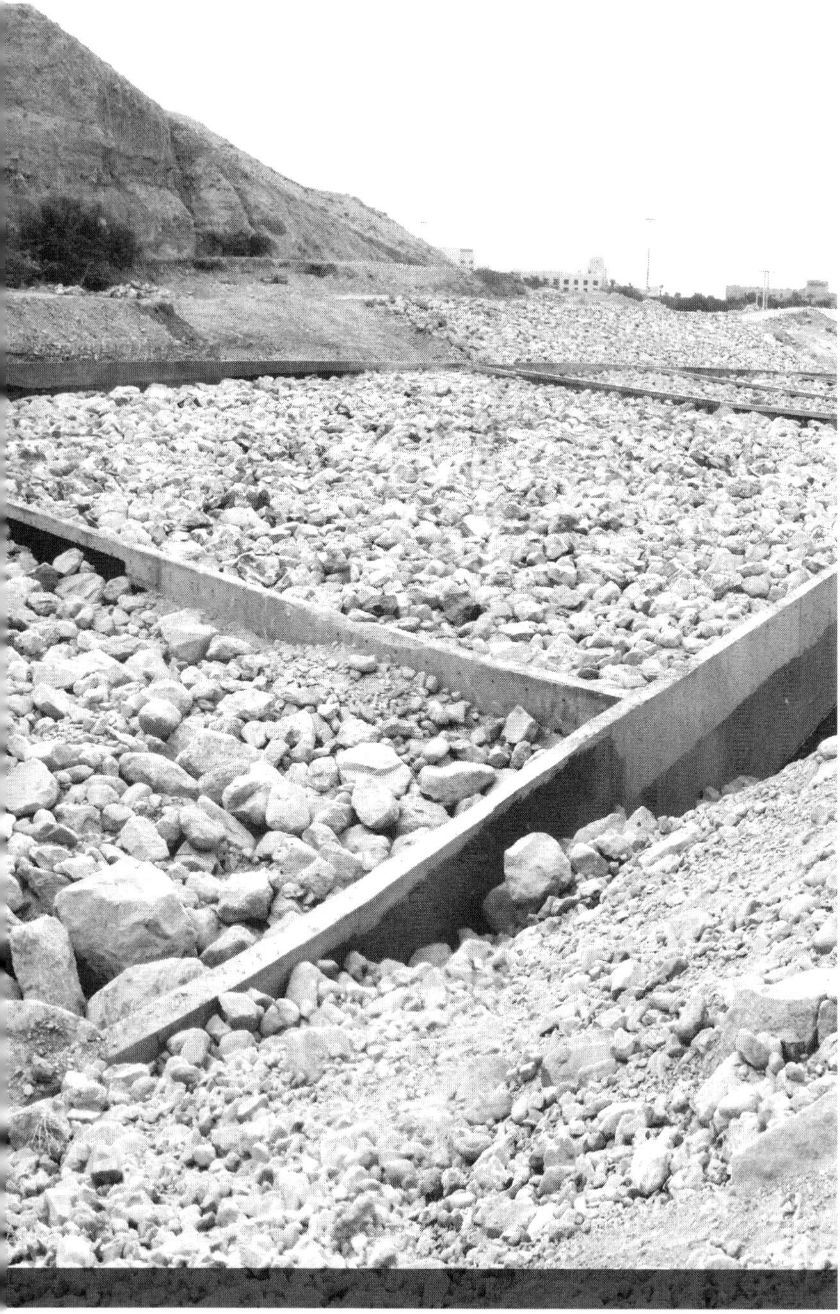

Wadi Numeira Siq Trail

Introduction

Located near the Dead Sea, this extraordinary wadi is famous for its hanging rock at the beginning of the trail and the magnificent and long narrow passage through the rock formation (the Siq). The wadi is known as "Water Petra" or Wadi Hudeira by the local Bedouins. It is an easy walk into a truly spectacular Siq with clear flowing water and massive walls that obscure the sky.

The trail can be reached easily with a 2WD car and is one of the hidden and easily accessible treasures in Jordan rarely visited by tourists. A guide or GPS device is not required to find your way on this easy 9 km (5.6 miles) trail in one of Jordan's impressive canyons.

Trail Description

After you have parked the car, walk under the massive hanging rock at the start of the trail. You will find yourself walking in water almost immediately, but the creek is shallow with a gravel bottom which provides good support. After walking in the creek for 800 m (0.5 miles) beyond the hanging rock, you enter an impressive Siq.

As you proceed, the Siq narrows and the cliffs extend above you to at least 100 m (328 ft.) with beautiful ochre and beef-colored sandstone. The wadi bed climbs steadily with an easy gradient. You will encounter one slightly awkward and slippery rock formation, while the few other boulders in the Siq can be navigated easier.

GPS FILE	21 WADI NUMEIRA SIQ TRAIL
Duration:	5 hours
Level:	Easy
Starting Point Coordinates:	N31 07.863 E35 31.981
Starting Point:	At the beginning of the wadi.
Is a Four Wheel Drive Car Required?	A 4x4 car is not required. You can park a normal car near the wadi.
Distance:	9.0 km (5.6 miles)
Highest Point:	-158 m (-518 ft.)
Lowest Point:	-325 m (-1,067 ft.)
Difference in Elevation:	167 m (549 ft.)
Trail Type:	Linear Trail (back and forth)
Is a GPS Device Required?	No
The Nearest Point with Amenities:	No services near the trail.

You will see stripes in the cliffs in a myriad of hues of red, orange and rust with streaks of fine conglomerate. The cliffs weave and wobble in a spectacular fashion such that the sky is blocked out completely. The Siq narrows to only a few meters in width, and the overhanging cliffs are beautiful and awe-inspiring. In summer, it is wonderfully cool.

A few hundred meters (500 ft.) on, the Siq widens. You will find yourself in a picturesque wadi with reeds, masses of tamarix and oleander seedlings and juniper. The cliffs become craggy, and you will see where a layer of soft sandstone about three meters (10 ft.) up supports a profusion of plants revealing where water is trickling out through the cliff. Keep an eye out for freshwater crabs. After 4.5 km (2.8 miles) along the trail, the wadi continues to the left, but you are past the best. Turn around in the wadi and retrace your steps to the car.

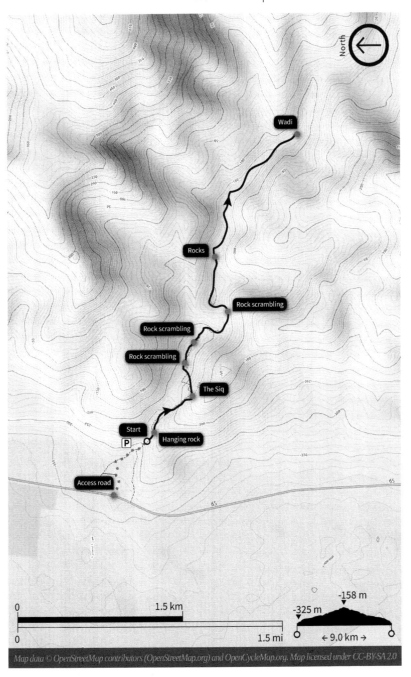

Getting There   *From Amman*

Starting at the 7th Circle in Amman, take Route 40 towards the Dead Sea for 45 km (28 miles) until it merges with the Dead Sea Highway (Route 65). Follow the Dead Sea Highway until you reach the Mujib Bridge and reset your odometer.

About 42 km (26 miles) south of the Wadi Mujib Bridge, on the Dead Sea Highway, look for a gravel road on the left 1 km (0.6 miles) past the Bromine factory. The gravel road is opposite a roadside monument which is on the right.

From Aqaba

Drive north from Aqaba on the Dead Sea Highway (Route 65) for about 2 hours passing the settlements of Rahma, Gharandal and Al Safi. You will pass the sign for "Lut's Cave" when the road curves to the left. From this point, continue for a further 8.9 km (5.5 miles) past the smokestacks of the Arab Potash Company and look for a gravel road on the right side of the Dead Sea Highway. There is a roadside monument opposite it on the left.

If you come to the Bromine factory, you have gone too far. Return and drive back for 1 km (0.6 miles) in the direction of Aqaba and make a left turn onto the gravel road near the roadside monument.

Continuing from both directions

Whether you come from Amman or Aqaba, follow the gravel road leading to an obvious chasm 600 m (0.4 miles) in front of you. Continue driving into the wadi past a huge acacia and park near the massive suspended rock (the "hanging rock") about 1 km (0.6 miles) from the road.

In the Siq

Trail Notes
- The trail is an easy walk along a wadi bed, with just one awkward slippery step to climb up.
- You can drive in the wadi with a 2WD.
- It can be busy on weekends with locals so be careful that you don't get parked in. Expect to be invited to drink tea with the families camping out near the beginning of the trail.
- You can download from *www.hiking-in-jordan.com* an E-trail that leads from the Dead Sea Highway to the beginning of the trail on the gravel road near the roadside monument. The file is named "21-1 Wadi Numeira Siq Trail Access Road Only."

Video Notes

0:16	-	The gravel road to the wadi.
0:38	-	The hanging rock at the beginning of the trail.
1:11	-	The one awkward step to climb up in the Siq. Unlike other boulders in the wadi, this smooth boulder is more challenging to navigate.
1:21	-	Entering the narrow passage of the Siq.
2:02	-	The wadi after the Siq.

The Dead Sea **Trail**
Wadi Weida'a

22

Introduction

Located not far from the salt evaporation ponds of Potash City on the Dead Sea Highway (Route 65) and the small historic site of Bab adh-Dhra'a (an early bronze age settlement), this is a short wadi walk through juniper, oleander, reeds and palms with a beautiful grotto and waterfall at the end.

A lovely and easy-to-reach canyon, Wadi Weida'a is a nice area for a family outing and those who enjoy waterfalls and an abundance of vegetation in a unique rocky desert landscape. Since this hike is relatively short (2.9 km, 1.8 miles), it can be easily combined with a visit to the castle in al-Karak.

You do not need a guide or GPS device for this trail.

Trail Description

From your car, follow a water conduit with the wadi below you on the left. Do not go into the wadi, but follow the conduit as it clings to the side of a cliff for about 200 m (656 ft.). The trail becomes a bit exposed here. Hug the cliff while you walk near the water conduit and clamber up the small dam wall to get to Wadi Weida.

From this point, it is a very easy and pleasant stroll up a palm-lined wadi with a running stream of clear water. Soon you will come to a tiny stone swimming pool on the right that is popular with local kids. Feel free to have a splash here if it isn't too busy.

The greenery thins out on the right as the cliff takes on vivid colors of sulphur, rust and rich browns

GPS FILE	22 WADI WEIDA'A
Duration:	2 hours
Level:	Easy
Starting Point Coordinates:	N31 14.568 E35 34.508
Starting Point:	The dam near the water station.
Is a Four Wheel Drive Car Required?	A 4x4 car is not required. You can park a normal car near the water station.
Distance:	2.9 km (1.8 miles)
Highest Point:	51 m (168 ft.)
Lowest Point:	-30 m (-99 ft.)
Difference in Elevation:	81 m (267 ft.)
Trail Type:	Linear Trail (back and forth)
Is a GPS Device Required?	No
The Nearest Point with Amenities:	No services near the trail. Al-Karak is the largest city in the vicinity of the hike.

caused by bacterial action and salt crystallization of seeping groundwater.

You stroll through lots of rushes, palms, tamarix and oleander until the wadi narrows to a very green glade with strange rock formations on the cliff above. This is a beautiful little grotto that is cool and shady with moist walls covered with maidenhair fern, palms, moss and pampas grass. It ends with a 4 m (13 ft.) waterfall pouring into a shallow, crystal clear pool with some of the cleanest water you will see in a wadi in Jordan.

When you have had your fill of this delightful place, head back down the wadi to your car for 1.5 km (0.9 miles).

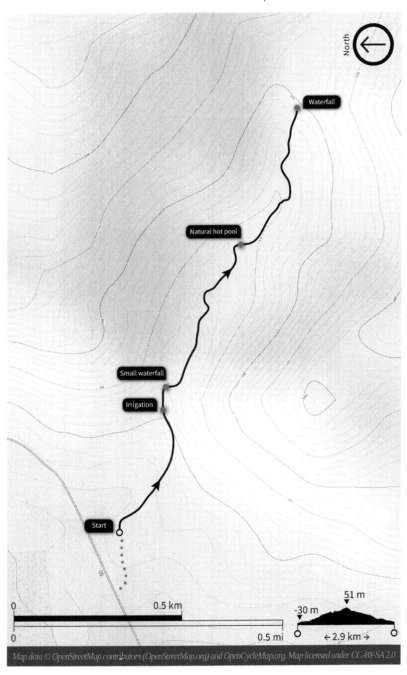

Getting There The wadi can be easily reached by car on Route 50 either from the direction of al-Karak or the Dead Sea Highway.

From Amman
Starting at the 7th Circle in Amman, take Route 40 towards the Dead Sea for 45 km (28 miles) until it merges with the Dead Sea Highway (Route 65). Follow the Dead Sea Highway until you reach the Mujib Bridge and reset your odometer. Drive for 25 km (15.6 miles) south to the turn-off on your left to al-Karak (Route 50). After 5.6 km (3.5 miles) turn right onto a short asphalt road near the wadi.

After 200 m (656 ft.), you can park next to a fence by a small reservoir with the wadi on your left.

From al-Karak
From the al-Karak castle, take Route 50 towards the Dead Sea and Potash City for 21.8 km (13.5 miles) and turn left onto an asphalt road. After 200 m (656 ft.), you can park next to a fence by a reservoir.

If you do not find the wadi, continue to the Dead Sea Highway on Route 50 from al-Karak. At the Dead Sea Highway, turn around and head back on Route 50 to al-Karak for 5.6 km (3.5 miles). Turn right on a short asphalt road near the wadi.

From Aqaba
While driving north from Aqaba on the Dead Sea Highway (Route 65), you will pass the settlements of Rahma, Gharandal and Al Safi. Drive for 2.5 hours (218 km or 135 miles) until you see the turn-off to al-Karak (Route 50) on the right, near Potash City.

Take the turn-off to al-Karak, drive 5.6 km (3.5 miles) and turn right on a short asphalt road before the wadi. After 200 m (656 ft.), you can park next to a fence by a reservoir with the wadi on your left.

- Do not expect to see much of Bab adh-Dhra'a just east of Potash City, since little is left of this early bronze age settlement. The al-Karak castle has much more to offer including cold drinks and a restaurant.
- A GPS file is included in our collection of E-trails that leads from the Dead Sea Highway to the turn-off point on Route 50. The file is named "22-1 Wadi Weida Access Road From Dead Sea."

Trail Notes

0:18	-	The wadi near the turn-off on Route 50. This is the starting point of the trail.
0:48	-	Follow the water conduit or irrigation channel towards the wadi.
1:00	-	The water conduit near the cliff.
2:02	-	Natural swimming pool popular with local kids.
2:30	-	The waterfall at the end of the trail.

Video Notes

Chris and Gregory at the End of the Trail

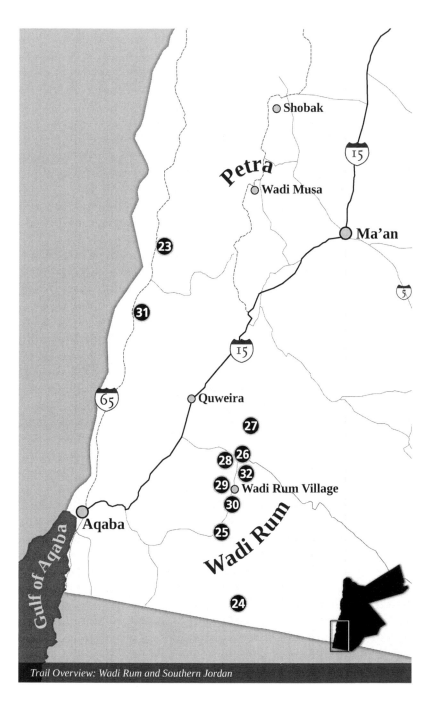

Trail Overview: Wadi Rum and Southern Jordan

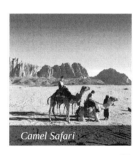

Camel Safari

Region
Wadi Rum and Southern Jordan

Wadi Rum and Southern Jordan
General Notes

Desert Lizard

In general, the following notes apply to the trails described in this section of the guide:

- Most trails are located in remote parts of Jordan, so make sure someone knows where you are and when you are expected back.
- Since most trails are rarely visited by tourists, unless you leave a note of your trip intentions it may be some time before a search is instigated if you find yourself in difficulties. Leave details with someone reliable of your trip intentions and expected time of return.
- You must be self-reliant. Don't expect a passer-by to assist as there are few visitors on most trails.
- Do not attempt to hike alone. It is wise to go with a group.
- There are no marked hiking trails, although evidence of the passage of other people is apparent for much of the way on a number of trails.
- There is no climbing involved or the need for ropes on any of the trails. Take care to pick the safest path.
- In summer, this area is very hot with temperatures exceeding 45 °C or 113 °F. Avoid the heat of the day in summer, carry water and use the available shade.
- We recommend that you hire a local guide on the advanced trails in case you need additional assistance during the hike.
- You need good shoes as there is some broken ground. Mostly you will have to contend with sand dunes and rough hills with some loose rocks.

Getting There Most trails in southern Jordan are located in Wadi Rum. It is easy to get there:

From Amman
Drive south on Route 15 (the Desert Highway), in the direction of Aqaba, passing Ma'an. After you have made the long descent into the valley, continue to drive south. You will pass the town of al-Quwayra (Quweira). The turn-off to Wadi Rum is 9.5 km (6 miles) south of this little town in the desert. The turn-off is well signposted.

From Aqaba
Drive north on Route 15 (the Desert Highway) and turn right from the Amman-Aqaba highway 42 km (26 miles) after the Aqaba customs check-point.

Continuing from both directions
Whether you come from the direction of Amman or Aqaba, getting to the Wadi Rum visitors' center is a straightforward 21 km (13 miles) from the turn-off on Route 15. Driving to Wadi Rum, you pass a railroad crossing 2.1 km (1.3 miles) from the turn off, and then a sign to the Bait Ali Lodge.

Access to the Trails in the Wadi Rum Reserve All trails in the Wadi Rum Reserve require that you buy an entrance ticket to the reserve at the visitors' center, including trails that start at the parking lot in Wadi Rum village.

Wadi Rum village is inside the reserve 7 km (4.4 miles) from the visitors' center.

Abu Barqa Dam Lookout

23

Introduction

This is an interesting little hike up a rocky wadi bed with fine views. There is plenty of opportunity to explore further here, but this is an isolated area so be self-reliant.

The dam is the starting point of a trail that leads through the wadi and to the top of a large sand dune which yields great views over Wadi Araba and Israel. The area is of interest to birdwatchers. You can spot Water Pipits, Green Sandpipers, Blackstarts, White-spectacled Bulbuls, Rock Martins and many other species if you are lucky. A GPS device or guide is not required to find your way to the dam, the wadi and the sand dunes near the end of the trail.

Trail Description

From your car, head straight up the river bed to the dam for 800 m (0.5 miles). Skirt around the dam, which is already heavily silted up by sediment carried by the floods. Continue to walk in the wadi, clambering over rounded river boulders. It can be slippery, so take care, especially if your boots get coated with the fine clay in the riverbed.

The walls climb steeply on either side, and the canyon winds to the right. Wade or portage the rock pools and continue until you reach a rather unexpected and very steep red sand dune on the right. You can continue to explore up the canyon if you wish, just return to the sand dune later. Climb the dune to attain a small ridge with views across Wadi Araba to the west. Then simply make your way north-west back down towards the creek bed and your car.

GPS FILE	23 ABU BARQA DAM LOOKOUT
Duration:	2.5 hours
Level:	Moderate
Starting Point Coordinates:	N30 09.549 E35 13.734
Starting Point:	The Abu Barqa Dam.
Is a Four Wheel Drive Car Required?	A 4x4 car is not required. You can park a normal car near the dam.
Distance:	3.9 km (2.4 miles)
Highest Point:	342 m (1,123 ft.)
Lowest Point:	212 m (694 ft.)
Difference in Elevation:	130 m (429 ft.)
Trail Type:	Circular Trail
Is a GPS Device Required?	No
The Nearest Point with Amenities:	No services near the trail.

Getting There

From Amman

Drive south on the Dead Sea Highway (Route 65) for 206 km (128 miles) from the 7th Circle in Amman and pass the Beir Mathkour rest house and gas station which is located on the right of the road. Zero your odometer at the gas station and drive a further 37.6 km (23.4 miles) south to enter a gravel/semi-paved road on the left. Follow the road towards the mountains and the sand dune for 2 km (1.2 miles). Park the car at the end of the road. If you see the turn-off to Rahma on the Dead Sea Highway, you have driven too far south. Turn around and drive 28.6 km (17.8 miles) north from the Rahma turn-off to the gravel road.

From Aqaba

If you are driving a 4X4 car, you can cross the river bed with stones and park on the left side of the river a couple of hundred meters further on.

Leave Aqaba heading for the Dead Sea Highway (Route 65). At the Wadi Araba customs check-point on the outskirts of Aqaba, zero your odometer. Drive north past the small town of Rahma and 57 km (35.4 miles) from the check-point turn right onto a gravel/

semi-paved road. This road is 28.6 km (17.8 miles) north of the turn-off to Rahma.

Follow this towards the mountains and the sand dune for 2 km (1.2 miles). Park the car at the end of the road.

About the Dam

- Based in Wadi Araba near the Dead Sea Highway (Route 65), the Abu Barqa Dam (also known as Abu Burqa Dam) has a storage capacity of around 500,000 m^3 of flood water from the nearby wadi, although the reservoir is heavily silted up by sediment carried by the floods.
- The dam was built as part of a community development program and provides irrigation water to farmers in Wadi Araba.
- The total construction cost of the dam was $1,376,000.

Trail Notes

- There is no path, with clambering over river boulders in sometimes slippery conditions. There is one steep dune to ascend.
- We recommend that you do not drink water from the wadi.
- Bring extra socks in case you need to walk through shallow water.
- The trail past the dam is isolated and is not frequently visited. Ensure someone knows where you are. Do not attempt to hike alone. It is wise to go with a group.
- Be aware of flash floods in the winter. Please do not hike in the wadi if it rains or has rained 24 hours prior to your planned hike.
- This can be a cold hike in winter and water levels may be hazardous. Check the weather and be prepared.

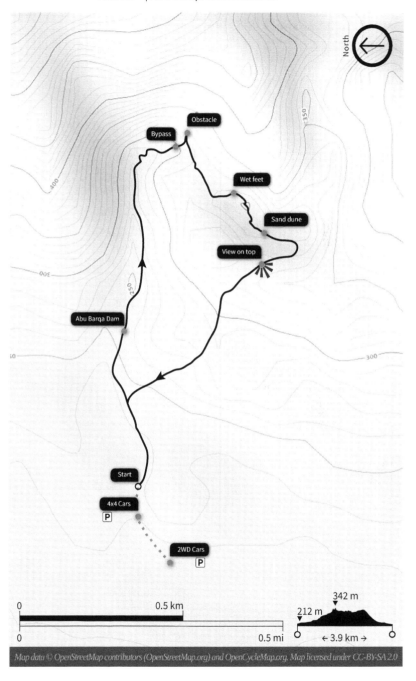

North

Obstacle

Bypass

Wet feet

Sand dune

View on top

Abu Barqa Dam

Start

4x4 Cars
P

2WD Cars
P

0   0.5 km

0   0.5 mi

342 m

212 m

← 3.9 km →

Video Notes

0:16 - Turn-off to the access road.

0:21 - A view of the area seen from the access road with the dam on the left and the large red sand dunes on the right.

0:50 - The Abu Barqa dam.

1:07 - The boulders you can expect in the wadi. You will have to navigate your way through the wadi. In our GPS E-trail, we have provided a few bypasses to avoid large boulders.

1:25 - The sand dune on the right side of the wadi.

1:35 - The point where we climbed up the sand dune.

2:00 - Magnificent views of Wadi Araba with Israel in the distance.

View over Wadi Araba, the Dam Basin and Israel from the Top of the Sand Dunes

Trail

Adami Trail - Jordan's Tallest Mountain

24

Jebel Um Adami, at 1,854 m (6,083 ft.) is the highest mountain in Jordan. It affords a fantastic panorama over the vast desert mountain ranges of southern Wadi Rum and north-western Saudi Arabia. The ascent is not difficult and takes only 1.5 to 2 hours of mostly easy walking with a little scrambling, but you need to be in good shape. You do not need special equipment or ropes to reach the summit.

Since the mountain is located in such an isolated location deep inside Wadi Rum, a GPS device or Bedouin guide is required to find the mountain and the summit.

Introduction

From where you park the car at the base of Jebel Um Adami, head west and pick your way up the slope to the first rise. Taking care, you can avoid any difficult clambering. From the first rise, there are good views back over where the car is parked to spectacular domes. It is worth a stop to catch your breath and enjoy it. Then head south-west (left) to attain a saddle.

Trail Description

From the saddle go east (left) and follow the ridge up. Pick the easiest path. Sometimes this will be to the right of the ridge rather than on the very top. Keep following the ridge as it curves to the summit. It is a relatively easy half hour hike to the top from this point.

Once up the top after 1.5 km (0.9 miles), you have a fantastic 360 degree panorama of a vast area of largely uninhabited Saudi Arabian and Jordanian

GPS FILE	24 ADAMI TRAIL - JORDAN'S TALLEST MOUNTAIN
Duration:	3 hours
Level:	Moderate
Starting Point Coordinates:	N29 18.586 E35 26.376
Starting Point:	Near the base of Adami Mountain.
Is a Four Wheel Drive Car Required?	Yes, Bedouins can arrange a 4X4 car easily.
Distance:	2.9 km (1.8 miles)
Highest Point:	1,854 m (6,083 ft.)
Lowest Point:	1,454 m (4,769 ft.)
Difference in Elevation:	400 m (1,314 ft.)
Trail Type:	Linear Trail (back and forth)
Is a GPS Device Required?	A GPS device or Bedouin guide is required to find the mountain and the summit.
The Nearest Point with Amenities:	No services near the trail.

deserts. The mountains seem to go endlessly. To the south-west you can even see the Gulf of Aqaba, 45 km (28 miles) away. It is worth stopping on the summit for a leisurely snack or lunch while you soak up the view. Remember you might not be back here again. If you sit quietly for a while, a small colony of Cairo spiny mice will usually appear from the rocks. They will appreciate your bread crust or apple core, as they rely on crumbs from the tourist trade.

After you have pondered the vastness of this epic landscape, your future hopes and aspirations, or what you are having for lunch, pick your way back down the ridge, remembering to turn right at the saddle and descend to the first rise where you will see your car waiting below.

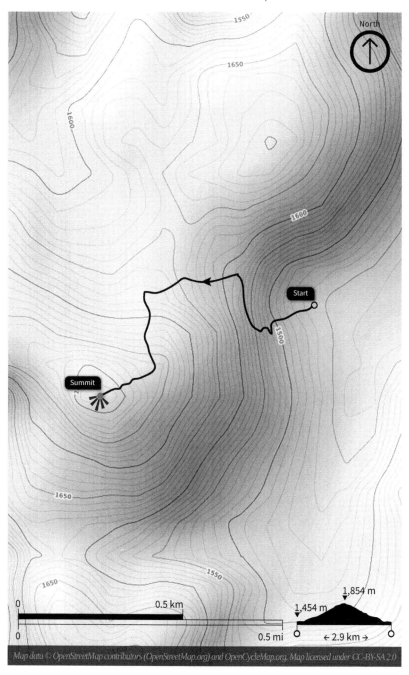

Geology Jebel Um Adami (sometimes written as Jabal Umm al Dami) is in spectacular country that is well worth visiting for the drive itself. You pass through a remote, wild and incredible landscape with beautiful light-colored domes of Disi sandstone.

The sandstones in Wadi Rum and elsewhere in Jordan are mainly of Palaeozoic (Cambrian to Silurian) age: 590 million to 408 million years old. Some younger, Lower Cretaceous, sandstones are 'only' 100-140 million years old.

There are three main types of sandstone in Jordan, each producing its own distinctive desert scenery. Hard, red sandstones (Cambrian age) form cliffs such as around Wadi Rum, white sandstones (Ordovician age) form domes, and soft, pink and white sandstones (Lower Cretaceous) form gentle slopes which you will see driving down to Jebel Um Adami.

Getting There Please see the general notes for Wadi Rum and southern Jordan for directions to the Wadi Rum visitors' center. Park your car in the Wadi Rum village parking lot to meet your Bedouin guide who can transport you to the mountain in a 4X4 car. If you travel independently, you can stop for a few supplies in Wadi Rum village if needed.

Remote Location Jebel Um Adami is deep inside the Wadi Rum Protected Area, 34.7 km (21.6 miles) south-east from Wadi Rum village. From Wadi Rum village, you'll need to follow the GPS track to find your way independently to the mountain. Since the location is so remote, we recommend that you hire a local guide, even if you elect to drive your own 4x4 car to the trail. It is best to arrange this in advance.

It is not a bad idea to camp out near the mountain as it is great country and you can hike early in the morning. This is less a choice and more an imperative during hot weather in the summer.

Chris on the Summit

The second highest peak in Jordan is Jebel Rum at 1,754 m (5,755 ft.). It was, in fact, the highest peak in Jordan until a land swap with Saudi Arabia in 1965 moved the Jordan-Saudi border south. This change increased Jordan's coastline on the Gulf of Aqaba by about 18 km (11.2 miles) to allow for port expansions and gained a fine mountain to boot.

Jebel Adami Compared to Jebel Rum

Jebel Um Adami is much easier to navigate than Jebel Rum, and the views are equally stunning and undoubtedly count as very good value for effort. While you can walk to the top of Adami, you will need climbing equipment and probably a guide from Wadi Rum village to climb to the summit of Jebel Rum.

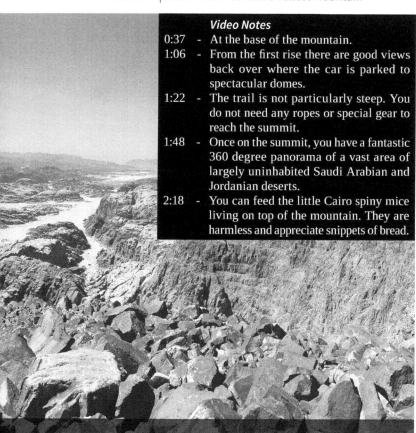

Video Notes

0:37 - At the base of the mountain.

1:06 - From the first rise there are good views back over where the car is parked to spectacular domes.

1:22 - The trail is not particularly steep. You do not need any ropes or special gear to reach the summit.

1:48 - Once on the summit, you have a fantastic 360 degree panorama of a vast area of largely uninhabited Saudi Arabian and Jordanian deserts.

2:18 - You can feed the little Cairo spiny mice living on top of the mountain. They are harmless and appreciate snippets of bread.

Trail Notes

- This is an isolated area with no local mobile phone reception (with international roaming you may pick up a Saudi mobile tower).
- You should be in a good 4X4 car and if without a guide you should be experienced in driving in soft sand and on rough ground and able to un-bog a car.
- A GPS file is included in our collection of E-trails that leads from Wadi Rum village to the base of the mountain. The file is named "24-1 Adami 4x4 Drive and Trail."
- You do not have to travel in the heart of Wadi Rum to the tallest mountain of Jordan for magnificent views. Also check out the Lawrence of Arabia Spring (» page 230).

Bedouin Camp Circuit

Introduction

Enjoy the sunset in the heart of Wadi Rum in the vicinity of Bedouin camps and the observatory. This is an easy hike that can be completed in less than three hours leading through Wadi Rum's spectacular landscapes. The trail is located in the Wadi Rum Reserve roughly 40 minutes' Jeep drive from Wadi Rum village.

To follow the trail exactly, you need to use the GPS E-trail. Alternatively, you can wander around using our map and trail description and explore the area if you do not mind deviating from the route.

Trail Description

This lovely circular trail starts in the middle of the Bedouin camps near the observatory. Although you can start the trail at any trail point, we start walking from one of our favorite camps: Salem Zalabih's "Mohammad Mutlak Camp." If you stay at other fine camps in the area, you can also start from the observatory which is 560 m (0.4 miles) north of Salem's camp.

From the camp, walk to the sand dune behind the tents and hug the rock formation on your left for 445 m (0.3 miles) until you see an opening through the rock formation on your left. Follow the opening while you are walking on the rock formation and descend into the little valley and climb again on the little hill ahead of you.

Turn right into a large valley as you walk towards the rock formation for 640 m (0.4 miles) and circumnav-

GPS FILE	25-1 BEDOUIN CAMP CIRCUIT
Duration:	2.5 hours
Level:	Easy
Starting Point Coordinates:	N29 29.237 E35 23.260
Starting Point:	Salem's Camp in the Wadi Rum Reserve.
Is a Four Wheel Drive Car Required?	Yes, Bedouins can arrange a 4X4 or camel safari easily.
Distance:	6.1 km (3.8 miles)
Highest Point:	1,070 m (3,511 ft.)
Lowest Point:	1,002 m (3,287 ft.)
Difference in Elevation:	68 m (224 ft.)
Trail Type:	Circular Trail
Is a GPS Device Required?	No, but recommended.
The Nearest Point with Amenities:	Bedouin camps in the vicinity have toilets and offer dinner.

igate the rock formation on your left for 850 m (0.5 miles) until you reach the mound on the right side of the rock formation in the valley.

From the mound, walk north-east for 450 m (0.3 miles) through an opening between two small rock formations and turn left while walking in a northerly direction as you pass a rock formation on your left. After 1.2 km (0.7 miles), you arrive at another rock formation. Find your way up the rock formation and descend west into the wadi to climb again on the rock formation ahead of you. At this point, you have arrived at the "Sunset Hill" from where you can see the observatory and the starting point of the trail.

From the Sunset Hill, find your way down to the desert and walk for 680 m (0.4 miles) to the observatory. The endpoint of the trail is 560 m (0.4 miles) south of the observatory.

Wadi Rum is one of the best places in Jordan for stargazing, due to its remoteness from big city lights, the clarity of the sky and the long horizon (range of 13 km, 8 miles). Astronomy is not new to Bedouins, as they have always been able to cross vast distances and deserts by relying on their knowledge of the stars.

The Observatory in Wadi Rum

The Aqaba Astronomy Association built an observatory near the Bedouin Camp Trail with support from the United States Agency for International Development (USAID) and in close consultation with the Bedouin Associations in Wadi Rum and Disi. The observatory has a 16" Meade Telescope and runs on solar panels. By providing job opportunities to young Bedouins as astronomy guides, the observatory supports Bedouin families in the area.

The Sky Gate Project

Please see the general notes for Wadi Rum and southern Jordan for directions to the Wadi Rum visitors' center.

Getting There

Park your car in the Wadi Rum village parking lot to meet your Bedouin guide who can transport you to the camp area in a 4X4 car.

Alternatively, you can book a camel to travel to the Bedouin camps from Wadi Rum village.

- Although you are in the vicinity of many Bedouin camps, this is an isolated area with limited mobile phone reception. Care must be taken here.
- The trail is located in the high-use zone of the Wadi Rum Reserve which permits vehicle tours, permanent campgrounds, rock climbing and other tourist activities. If you get lost, the Bedouins will look after you.

Trail Notes

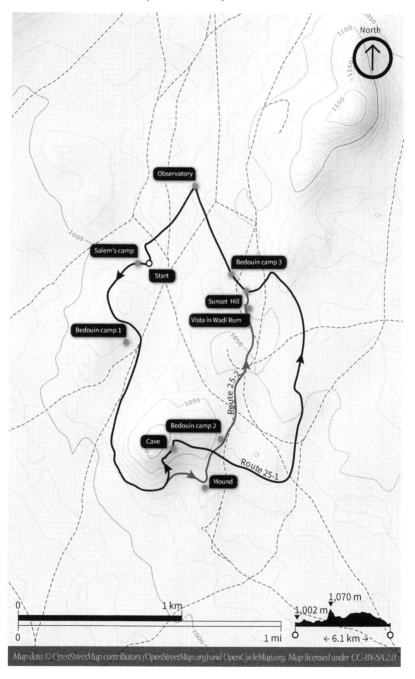

Jeep Safari

Video Notes

0:20	-	Salem's "Mohammed Mutlak Camp", the starting point of the trail.
0:58	-	There are no clearly marked paths to follow the trail. We recommend that you bring a GPS device with the E- trail.
1:10	-	You will see a number of other Bedouin camps from the trail.
1:40	-	Truly magnificent views of Wadi Rum.
2:05	-	The "Sunset Hill" near the observatory.
2:20	-	The observatory in Wadi Rum near the end point of the trail.

This is a shorter version of the Bedouin Camp Circuit Trail. Using the GPS E-trail, you will end up at the Sunset Hill and the observatory, while you by-pass the rock formation east.

Extended - Alternative E-trail Version

GPS FILE	25-2 BEDOUIN CAMP CIRCUIT
Duration:	2 hours
Level:	Easy
Starting Point Coordinates:	N29 29.237 E35 23.260
Starting Point:	Salem's Camp in the Wadi Rum Reserve.
Is a Four Wheel Drive Car Required?	Yes, Bedouins can arrange a 4X4 or camel safari easily.
Distance:	5.3 km (3.3 miles)
Highest Point:	1,064 m (3,490 ft.)
Lowest Point:	1,005 m (3,296 ft.)
Difference in Elevation:	59 m (194 ft.)
Trail Type:	Circular Trail
Is a GPS Device Required?	No, but recommended.
The Nearest Point with Amenities:	Bedouin camps in the vicinity have toilets and offer dinner.

Wadi Rum and Southern Jordan

26 Burial Mound and Oryx Trail

Introduction Wadi Rum is a popular place for climbing and Jeep tours, but is seriously under rated when it comes to hiking. The Burial Mound and Oryx Trail is a spectacular hike that leads through an area that is rarely visited by tourists and even Bedouins.

There is a fair bit of scrambling and rock hopping involved, and while none of it is particularly difficult, it requires reasonable physical fitness. In addition to the physical challenges, this hike also requires additional preparation.

While the trail is close to the Wadi Rum visitors' center, it is in an isolated area with little or no mobile phone reception, and you are unlikely to encounter assistance if needed. Care must be taken here, as this trail cannot be followed without a GPS device loaded with our E-trail. Hiking in this part of Wadi Rum is superb, but there are no marked trails.

You could easily overnight on this hike and do some exploring, but you'll need to be self-reliant in everything including water.

Trail Description The trail starts at the Wadi Rum visitors' center. From the visitors' center, start to head south on the road to Wadi Rum village. As soon as you are past the hill immediately on your right (only after 200 m, 656 ft.) turn south-west (right) into Wadi el Sid.

While you are facing the wadi (to the south), you see a mountain range that extends from the east (left) by

GPS FILE	26-1 BURIAL MOUND AND ORYX TRAIL
Duration:	6 hours
Level:	Advanced
Starting Point Coordinates:	N29 38.363 E35 26.054
Starting Point:	Wadi Rum visitors' center.
Is a Four Wheel Drive Car Required?	A 4x4 car is not required. You can park a normal car at the visitors' center.
Distance:	14.5 km (9.0 miles)
Highest Point:	1,180 m (3,872 ft.)
Lowest Point:	828 m (2,716 ft.)
Difference in Elevation:	352 m (1,156 ft.)
Trail Type:	Circular Trail
Is a GPS Device Required?	Yes
The Nearest Point with Amenities:	The visitors' center has toilets, shops and a restaurant.

the Wadi Rum road to the head of Wadi el Siq on the right (note this is where you will come from later in this hike). Make for the main gully that cuts through the mountain range about halfway along its length. Ignore the smaller gully to the left of it. As you get closer, you'll see two distinctive conspicuous black bands of basalt in the red sandstone on the right of the gully confirming this is the right one.

Enter the gully and follow it as it leads you first south and then west. The gully is an interesting jumble of river stones and boulders with a few scattered tamarix. There is some rock hopping to be enjoyed, just mind your step and remember to stop to look back to enjoy the view as you climb the gully. Watch for rock geckos basking in the sun. There are Nubian Ibex in this area, but you'll have to be quiet and very vigilant to have any chance of spotting one.

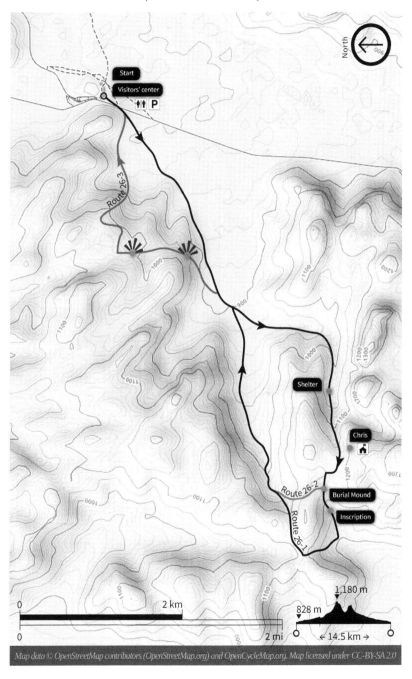

Keep following the gully west, ignoring a side-gully to the south (left). When you come to a small cliff marking the end of the gully, skirt it to the right where there is a bit of a path that provides the easiest ascent. This gets you to a saddle offering fine views back east towards the Seven Pillars of Wisdom and the visitors' center from whence you have come.

From the saddle, go westwards (straight ahead) a couple of hundred meters then drop down to the north (right) into a small valley. Now turn west (left) to find an intact burial mound on a saddle at N29 36.868 E35 23.262. From the burial mound saddle, there are two options to continue:

Route 26-1: Drop straight down on the rocky slope ahead to the west, minding your step in the loose stones. Turn north-west (right), making for the saddle there, then cut across and pick your way north-east (right) to another saddle which affords views to the north and east back towards the Seven Pillars of Wisdom.

On the way down on Route 26-1, look for the spooky caverns in the cliffs to the right (a formation known as tafoni).

Route 26-2: The alternative way from the burial mound is shorter and with better views, but is slightly harder. Head north up the slope to gain a rocky ridge. The views are spectacular. Head north-west along the top of the ridge until almost the end (about 400 m, 0.2 miles) then look for a way down to a saddle to the north side. There are safe paths down; take your time to find one.

Please note that an E-trail for Route 26-2 is not available. You will need to navigate from the BM-Burial Mound GPS waypoint at N29 36.868 E35 23.262 to BM-Trail Point 8 at N29 37.146 E35 23.124 which is an easy thing to do. Whichever path you choose, you will eventually end up at BM-Trail Point 8.

Once down in Wadi el Sid, simply keep going east

then north-east to arrive back at the visitors' center, or head to where you left your car.

Getting There Please see the general notes for Wadi Rum and southern Jordan for directions to the Wadi Rum visitors' center.

Trail Notes Although the trail starts in the vicinity of the Wadi Rum visitors' center, this is an isolated area with no mobile phone reception. Care must be taken here.

Extended / Alternative Version Additionally, if you have energy to burn, you can combine the trail with the Ibex Canyon Lookout *(» page 222)* and fit in a bit more for the day. Please only attempt to combine these trails if you are in very good shape. Please check out the GPS E-trail for more information on this hike.

GPS FILE	26-3 BURIAL MOUND AND ORYX TRAIL-TO IBEX LOOKOUT
Duration:	8 hours
Level:	Advanced
Starting Point Coordinates:	N29 38.363 E35 26.054
Starting Point:	Wadi Rum visitors' center.
Is a Four Wheel Drive Car Required?	A 4x4 car is not required. You can park a normal car at the visitors' center.
Distance:	16.3 km (10.1 miles)
Highest Point:	1,180 m (3,872 ft.)
Lowest Point:	828 m (2,716 ft.)
Difference in Elevation:	352 m (1,156 ft.)
Trail Type:	Circular Trail
Is a GPS Device Required?	Yes
The Nearest Point with Amenities:	The visitors' center has toilets, shops and a restaurant.

Burial Mound

Video Notes

0:13 - The Wadi Rum visitors' center. Park your car at the visitors' center, buy your ticket and follow the road to Wadi Rum village for 200 m (656 ft.) to make a right turn.

0:34 - Animation explaining the trail. You cannot hike this trail without the GPS E-trail unless you are familiar with the terrain. The animation shows Route 26-1 of the trail.

0:46 - Enter the gully here.

0:51 - The gully is an interesting jumble of river stones and boulders with a few scattered tamarix.

1:33 - The burial mound. From this point you have two options to continue the trail.

French Fortress Trail

27

This hiking trail starts at the fortress once used for the 2001 French game show "The Desert Forges." The fortress is well maintained and is situated in the vicinity of the Bait Ali Lodge in one of Jordan's most beautiful desert landscapes that are seen by few tourists.

Introduction

The hike passes through a popular picnic area for Bedouin families who enjoy the spectacular views on Fridays. Be prepared to accept a cup of tea when

The Fortress

you are 30 minutes into the hike. You will see stunning views, a gigantic sand dune and the famous Mushroom Rock on this wonderful hike.

The trail is outside the Wadi Rum Reserve. You do not need to purchase a ticket to hike this trail. A GPS device is required to follow the trail.

Trail Description Walk from the fortress heading south-west, towards the large sand dune ahead of you and scale the small rock outcrops along the trail to get fine views to the east.

Once you scale the dune, cross onto a second dune and bear right up the peak to reach the rocks. Following the edge, head south-east (left), and you will come to a viewpoint next to a mushroom rock (although this rock is an imposter - it is not the real Mushroom Rock you will see later on the trail).

After you take in the view, backtrack a bit heading south-west and pass between two peaks with a red

GPS FILE	27 FRENCH FORTRESS TRAIL
Duration:	3.5 hours
Level:	Moderate
Starting Point Coordinates:	N29 43.657 E35 28.380
Starting Point:	The French Fortress.
Is a Four Wheel Drive Car Required?	No, unless the access road is covered with sand.
Distance:	11.1 km (6.9 miles)
Highest Point:	882 m (2,893 ft.)
Lowest Point:	786 m (2,577 ft.)
Difference in Elevation:	96 m (316 ft.)
Trail Type:	Circular Trail
Is a GPS Device Required?	Yes
The Nearest Point with Amenities:	No services near the trail.

dune between them. You will tramp through sand with a lot of rocks, vegetated with anabasis, hammada and retama shrubs. Descend on the other side of the dune into a fine canyon with "dripping wax" cliffs. Look for Sooty Falcons here.

At the bottom, follow the cliffs around to the left, passing an attractive dune. You will come to the "official" Mushroom Rock. There is normally a Bedouin tent here with tea and trinkets.

From the Mushroom Rock, backtrack a bit to head back north, and trend north-west up a large valley with a very big and spectacular rock formation on your left. After about 2.5 km (1.6 miles) as the rock formation comes to an end, go through the gap between this massif and a small outcrop. You then come onto a distinctively paler, more orange, and very beautiful dune.

The view of the plain to the west and north is ab-

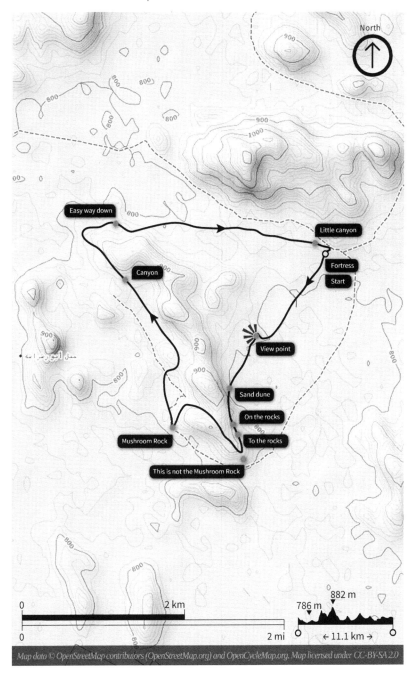

Massive Sand Dunes

solutely superb. Turn east (right) onto a red/pink dune, passing a massive outcrop on your right with impressive vertical slabs. Ascend a small rise to find yourself on a massive and very steep dune. The views are awe-inspiring from here, and the golden yellow sands are stunning. You can see the French Fortress in the distance to the east (right) at the far end of the valley below. When you are ready, descend the dune to the valley floor and head up the valley to return to the fortress and your vehicle.

From Amman Getting There

Drive south on Route 15 (the Desert Highway), in the direction of Aqaba, passing Ma'an. After you have made the long descent into the valley, continue to drive south. You will pass the town of al-Quwayra (Quweira). The turn-off to Wadi Rum is 9.5 km (6 miles) south of this little town in the desert.

The turn-off to Wadi Rum is well signposted. While driving in the direction of Wadi Rum, you will pass a railroad crossing after 2.1 km (1.3 miles).

From Aqaba

Drive north on Route 15 (the Desert Highway), and turn right of the Amman-Aqaba highway 42 km (26 miles) after the Aqaba customs check-point. The turn-off to Wadi Rum is well signposted. While driving in the direction of Wadi Rum, you will pass a railroad crossing after 2.1 km (1.3 miles).

Continuing from both directions

Whether you come from the direction of Amman or Aqaba, getting to the turn-off to the French Fortress is a straightforward 10.8 km (6.7 miles) from the railroad crossing. The turn-off is on your left and you will need to cross the railroad track again. If you see the sign to the Bait Ali Lodge near a path on the left crossing the railroad, you have driven too far. Turn around and take the first road that crosses the railroad track on your right.

Follow the dirt road to the French Fortress for 10.5 km (6.5 miles). If the dirt road is not covered by drift sand, you can drive to the French Fortress with a normal car. If you get stuck, you can always park the car as far as you can drive and walk to the closest GPS E-trail point.

About the Fortress
- The "Fortress" was built as a set for a French TV game show. It is periodically used for movie shoots. There is a caretaker who may be present.
- It is worth spending half an hour exploring the place if the caretaker lets you. The walkways along the top of the buildings are evocative of western movies. Intriguing staircases lead nowhere in particular and you'll find yourself in a futuristic place. There is even a set depicting a mine.

Trail Notes
- You can download from *www.hiking-in-jordan.com* an E-trail that leads from the Wadi Rum road to the beginning of the trail at the French Fortress. The file is named "27-1 French Fortress Trail with Access Road Track."
- South of the French Fortress is a barren clay flat. Wadi Rum is in the distance to the south; you can see Jebel Rum on the right and Jebel um Ishrin on the left.

Video Notes

0:17	-	The French Fortress.
0:34	-	The large sand dune.
1:32	-	This is the imposter Mushroom Rock! Great views though.
1:58	-	The "official" Mushroom Rock near a Bedouin camp.
2:15	-	At the end of the trail near the French Fortress.

Ibex Canyon Lookout

Introduction

This is a spectacular hike close to the Wadi Rum visitors' center that provides superb views of the Seven Pillars of Wisdom and escapes the crowds within minutes. The walk can be cut short easily, and stunning views can be gained with a one hour round trip if you backtrack down the trail. But if you have the time, the circuit is well worth it as you will get some of the best views Wadi Rum has to offer.

While the trail is close to the Wadi Rum visitors' center, it is in an isolated area with little or no mobile phone reception, and you are unlikely to encounter assistance if needed. Care must be taken here, as this trail cannot be followed without a GPS device loaded with our E-trail. Hiking in this part of Wadi Rum is superb, but there are no marked trails.

Trail Description

From the visitors' center, walk through the gate south on the road towards Wadi Rum village for 330 m (0.2 miles) and turn west (right) and follow a dry creek into the valley. As you round the hill on your right, you will see a sheer-sided mountain to the west (the one standing highest from the others looking from this vantage point). This is where you are heading.

You will pass a small knob of rock. Keep going and aim for a faint gully in line with the left-hand-side of the sheer-sided mountain. One branch of the creek leads directly to this gully. Ascend this gully to the saddle, then turn right and head up the ridge of dark basement basaltic rock.

Chris in Action on the Trail

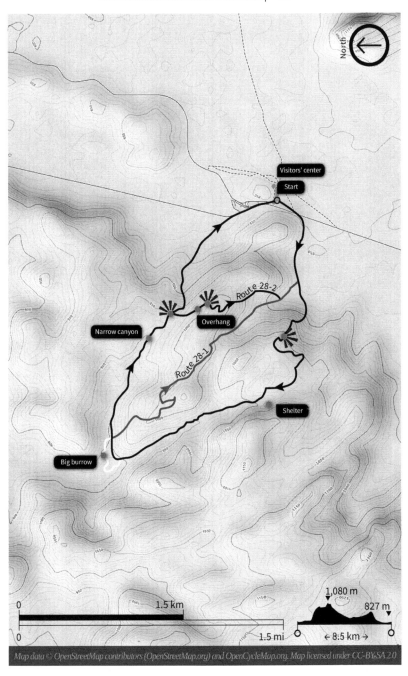

GPS FILE	28 IBEX CANYON LOOKOUT
Duration:	5 hours
Level:	Advanced
Starting Point Coordinates:	N29 38.380 E35 26.045
Starting Point:	Wadi Rum visitors' center.
Is a Four Wheel Drive Car Required?	A 4x4 car is not required. You can park a normal car at the visitors' center.
Distance:	8.5 km (5.3 miles)
Highest Point:	1,080 m (3,544 ft.)
Lowest Point:	827 m (2,713 ft.)
Difference in Elevation:	253 m (831 ft.)
Trail Type:	Circular Trail
Is a GPS Device Required?	Yes
The Nearest Point with Amenities:	The visitors' center has toilets, shops and a restaurant.

You will come to a red sandstone bluff. Skirt around the east side of it (i.e., walk around to the right) then you can ascend part way up the north-east side of the bluff (i.e., go up to the left). Don't forget to enjoy the fine views behind you as you climb. Skirt back south around the east side of the bluff again heading to the left or climb to the top if you have the energy and soak up even more excellent views. Assuming you skirt around the bluff, simply head on towards the right hand side of the steep sided mountain, crossing a short flat on your way and coming to a red sand dune. If you went up the top, pick your way along the ridge over fairly rough terrain until you get to the red sand dune by the steep-sided mountain.

From the dune, head south (left) and keep roughly the same contour as you clamber around the east side of the mountain. You will round a headland. Around the other side, skirt the boulder pile then hug the base of the sheer yellow cliffs to continue west around the southern side of the mountain. You have now completed one-third of the trail.

When you come to the north-western side of the mountain (past the cliffs), drop down into the valley to the south-west (left) and follow the creek bed to the bottom, heading north-west. You'll come to a lovely sheltered valley with wadis entering from several directions. You need to turn immediately right into the wadi heading north and follow the creek bed up. You are now halfway along the trail.

When the creek bed branches, go left. It turns to the east and then south-east as it climbs. Look for a small rocky hill at the top with exceptional views to the north and east. You can see the visitors' center from here.

To get back to the visitors' center, head down the gully on your right. Take care as there is a lot of loose material until you are clear of the sandstone.

The Nubian Ibex

The mountains in the hiking area are a refuge of the Nubian Ibex (*Capra nubiana*). Inaccessible mountains such as those around Wadi Rum are the only reason the nimble Ibex maintains its tenuous hold in Jordan. Unfortunately, Ibex suffer from relentless hunting, even inside the Wadi Rum Protected Area. The culprits are equipped with powerful rifles, superb hunting skills, patience and a hunger for game meat. Nonetheless, it is possible to see Ibex if you are watchful and quiet. It is not hard to see signs of Ibex presence including tracks and scats, which you should be able to see on this hike especially under overhangs.

Getting There

Please see the general notes for Wadi Rum and southern Jordan for directions to the Wadi Rum visitors' center.

Trail Notes

Although the trail starts in the vicinity of the Wadi Rum visitors' center, this is an isolated area with no mobile phone reception. Care must be taken here.

Extended - Alternative E-trail Versions If you are interested in an additional workout and do not mind some serious rock scrambling, we have two additional variations of the Ibex Canyon Lookout Trail. The E-trails are more demanding and longer both in time and in distance. Check out the GPS E-trails for more information on the alternative routes.

GPS FILE	28-1 IBEX CANYON LOOKOUT ROCK SCRAMBLING	28-2 IBEX CANYON LOOKOUT ROCK SCRAMBLING
Duration:	5.5 hours	6 hours
Level:	Advanced	Advanced
Starting Point Coordinates:	N29 38.380 E35 26.045	N29 38.380 E35 26.045
Starting Point:	Wadi Rum visitors' center.	Wadi Rum visitors' center.
Is a Four Wheel Drive Car Required?	A 4x4 car is not required. You can park a normal car at the visitors' center.	A 4x4 car is not required. You can park a normal car at the visitors' center.
Distance:	9.5 km (5.9 miles)	10.3 km (6.4 miles)
Highest Point:	1,073 m (3,519 ft.)	1,073 m (3,519 ft.)
Lowest Point:	839 m (2,754 ft.)	846 m (2,776 ft.)
Difference in Elevation:	234 m (765 ft.)	227 m (743 ft.)
Trail Type:	Circular Trail	Circular Trail
Is a GPS Device Required?	Yes	Yes
The Nearest Point with Amenities:	The visitors' center has toilets, shops and a restaurant.	The visitors' center has toilets, shops and a restaurant.

The Seven Pillars of Wisdom in the Distance

Video Notes

0:21 - The Wadi Rum visitors' center.

0:28 - The trail starts at the Wadi Rum visitors' center.

1:11 - The kind of terrain you can expect on this trail.

1:18 - You will be rewarded with magnificent views of Wadi Rum.

1:23 - You will see the Seven Pillars of Wisdom from a distance.

1:29 - The red sand dune by the steep-sided mountain.

Lawrence of Arabia Spring

Introduction

This hike is very picturesque and takes you to a lovely spring that T.E. Lawrence actually visited, unlike the numerous sham Lawrence locations about the place (including another commercialized "Lawrence Spring" which is located south of Wadi Rum village).

This hike also affords great views of Wadi Rum village.

Shallow paved steps help you navigate the hillside towards the spring. A picnic area has been built near the top of the path that leads to the spring. Once you are at the spring, follow the trail along the hillside towards a magnificent vista. A guide or GPS device is not required.

Trail Description

The trail starts at the parking lot in Wadi Rum village from where the Nabatean temple can be seen. From the temple site, it is 30 minutes to the Ain Shallalah spring, which is the "Real Lawrence of Arabia Spring." The spring fed the Nabatean temple and village area.

From the parking lot, walk directly towards the temple which is only five minutes away. If you use our GPS E-trail, we have built in a little detour that leads to the small passage to the right when you walk towards the temple.

Once you have explored the temple, head south for 0.6 km (0.4 miles) to the stone steps that lead to the spring. As you walk towards the steps, you have the

GPS FILE	29 LAWRENCE OF ARABIA SPRING (AIN SHALLALAH)
Duration:	2.5 hours
Level:	Moderate, although going to the spring only is an easy hike on a well established path.
Starting Point Coordinates:	N29 34.694 E35 25.172
Starting Point:	Wadi Rum village.
Is a Four Wheel Drive Car Required?	A 4x4 car is not required. You can park a normal car in the village's parking lot.
Distance:	4.8 km (3.0 miles)
Highest Point:	1,086 m (3,563 ft.)
Lowest Point:	951 m (3,120 ft.)
Difference in Elevation:	135 m (443 ft.)
Trail Type:	Circular Trail
Is a GPS Device Required?	No
The Nearest Point with Amenities:	Wadi Rum village has toilets, shops and restaurants.

mountain on your right and the village on your left. The steps are located near an asphalt road that leads back to the village.

When you're facing the stone steps that lead up to the spring, the Nabatean temple is to your right and the village is behind you.

The steps take you to a good vantage point 2.7 km (1.7 miles) from the parking area overlooking Wadi Rum village and the Um Ishrin range behind it. This is a fine place for a picnic or rest stop. Continuing on, the path contours around and passes several springs. There are caper vines hanging from the cliffs and fig trees and mint, which seem luxuriant compared to the desert behind you. You will find shady places offering welcome respite from the heat in the summer.

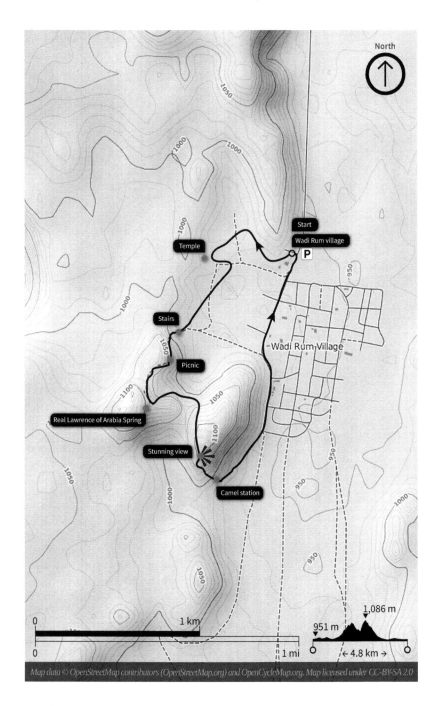

North

Temple

Start
Wadi Rum village

P

Stairs

Wadi Rum Village

Picnic

950

Real Lawrence of Arabia Spring

Stunning view

Camel station

1 km

1 mi

951 m

1,086 m

← 4.8 km →

Follow the path to the end where water trickles from an overhang into puddles in the shade. This is the area Lawrence describes in his book:

"In the idleness forced on him by our absence, Lewis had explored the cliff, and reported the springs very good for washing in; so, to get rid of the dust and strain after my long rides, I went straight up the gully into the face of the hill, along the ruined wall of the conduit by which a spout of water had once run down the ledges to a Nabatasan well-house on the valley floor. It was a climb of fifteen minutes to a tired person, and not difficult. At the top, the waterfall, el Shellac as the Arabs named it, was only a few yards away."

T.E. Lawrence, The Seven Pillars of Wisdom

From here, either return the way you came, or continue on for the full hike. To do so, head left of the springs along the base of the cliff. About 20 m (66 ft.) along you will see the remains of a Nabatean carved stone causeway that once channeled water down the hill. There are pieces of causeway all the way down the hill.

Since there is no clear path that you can follow, you will need to find your way through the boulders. Initially you may have to go down on the slope a bit on the left before you can find a way up to the right as you walk along the steep cliff on the right.

Continue along the cliff heading east, finding your way along and up the slope until you come to a wide gully on your right. Make a right turn into the gully and follow it to the top. Your effort will be rewarded with a truly magnificent vista towards the mountains of Khazali (on the left) and Qata (on the right).

To get back to the car from this view point, you have two options:

1 Turn around and go back down the gully you just came up. Follow it to the bottom, then pick your way past the little gardens to your car at the parking lot.

2 Continue the hike down into the valley on your left scrambling through the rocks. Once you are in the valley, make a left turn and walk towards Wadi Rum village. You will pass a camel station on the left side. After 0.6 km (0.4 miles), you are back on the asphalt road in Wadi Rum village that leads to the public parking area.

Getting There

Please see the general notes for Wadi Rum and southern Jordan for directions to the Wadi Rum visitors' center and Wadi Rum village.

About the Nabatean Temple and the Ain Shallalah Spring

- The Ain Shallalah Spring is described in the Seven Pillars of Wisdom: A Triumph by T. E. Lawrence ("Lawrence of Arabia") who served as a British liaison officer during the Arab Revolt from 1916 to 1918 against the Ottoman Turks.
- Lawrence never saw the nearby Nabatean settlement: It was discovered in Wadi Rum by Savignac in 1932. Savignac and Horsfield undertook the first excavations in 1933 and recorded Nabatean, Greek and Thamudic inscriptions and graffiti at the temple and at Ain Shallalah.
- You can read more about the Nabatean Temple in the description of the Nabatean Temple Trail *(» page 236)*.

Trail Notes

- Bedouin guides tend to skip the authentic Lawrence of Arabia Spring and have declared what they nowadays call "the Lawrence Spring" to be the real one, so they can easily transport tourists by car avoiding the 30 minute walk on the steps to the real spring. This explains why very few people actually visit the real spring.
- If you cannot find your way to the steps to the real Lawrence of Arabia Spring, don't hesitate to ask a local Bedouin for directions to "Ain Shallalah" where the steps are. It's an eight-minute walk from Wadi Rum village to the steps. No Jeep ride or guide is needed.

Video Notes

0:22 - Wadi Rum village.

0:27 - Near the steps that lead to the authentic Lawrence of Arabia Spring.

1:07 - This is how the steps look like on the trail.

1:54 - You will pass several smaller springs before you end up at the last spring which is the real Lawrence of Arabia Spring.

2:23 - The gully that leads up to the top for magnificent views of Wadi Rum.

2:32 - This is possibly one of the best views in Wadi Rum located conveniently near the Wadi Rum village. If you do not have the time or appetite to travel to Jebel Adami for spectacular views from Jordan's tallest mountain (» page 194), the Lawrence of Arabia Spring Trail is a valuable alternative that can be easily included during a short visit to Wadi Rum.

Camel Holding Place Near the Trail

Wadi Rum and Southern Jordan

Nabatean Temple Trail

Located near the village in Wadi Rum, this wonderful trail leads through two valleys with a spring, vegetation and palm trees. It affords fine views of the village, the Nabatean temple, the surrounding mountains and the wadi itself. You can turn back at any point, and even a small walk up the ridge is well worth it as it yields a plethora of excellent photo opportunities.

Introduction

The trail is near the Wadi Rum village parking lot and does not require a guide or GPS device.

Wadi Rum Village Seen from the Trail

Trail Description Head straight up a small gully at the end of the main parking lot in the beginning of Wadi Rum village. It veers left a little. Keep going up until you are on top of a small ridge that looks back over the car park. Turn left to follow this ridge up. Before you reach the top, walk to the right to a saddle. On the saddle, you will encounter some exposed burial mounds to have a look at.

Cross the saddle heading north more or less straight ahead leaving behind Wadi Rum village. You immediately come to a huge orange rock that looks like a ship's bow. Keep left of this rock and keep to the right of the next bluff. After 20 m (72 ft.) climb a small gully. You will reach a shingle plateau on top of the ridge. There are a couple more burial mounds here.

Follow this ridge as it curves towards the west (left). Instead of climbing the next outcrop, drop down a little to the right and skirt the outcrop on its east side under an overhang. This leads around to a small saddle. Immediately after you go through this saddle veer right. Keep the ridge to your right. Head towards

GPS File	30 Nabatean Temple Trail
Duration:	3.5 hours
Level:	Moderate
Starting Point Coordinates:	N29 34.694 E35 25.172
Starting Point:	Wadi Rum village.
Is a Four Wheel Drive Car Required?	A 4x4 car is not required. You can park a normal car in the village's parking lot.
Distance:	5.5 km (3.4 miles)
Highest Point:	1,072 m (3,517 ft.)
Lowest Point:	930 m (3,050 ft.)
Difference in Elevation:	142 m (467 ft.)
Trail Type:	Circular Trail
Is a GPS Device Required?	No. A GPS device with the E-trail is recommended to follow the exact route, unless you skip most of the rock scrambling part and you stay mostly in the valley.
The Nearest Point with Amenities:	Wadi Rum village has toilets, shops and restaurants.

the rock formation to the west until you are in a third saddle. From the saddle, head north (right) down a small gully and keep the rock formation to your left as you veer to the north-west (left) up onto saddle number four.

From here, you exit down the gully and descend into the valley on your left. Head north up the main gully (walking away from the direction of the Nabatean temple) towards the oasis. Follow the gully up to the saddle, find your way down in the valley on a steep rock formation (you need to slide down) and follow a gully to the right. From this point, it is 2.7 km (1.7 miles) to the car park.

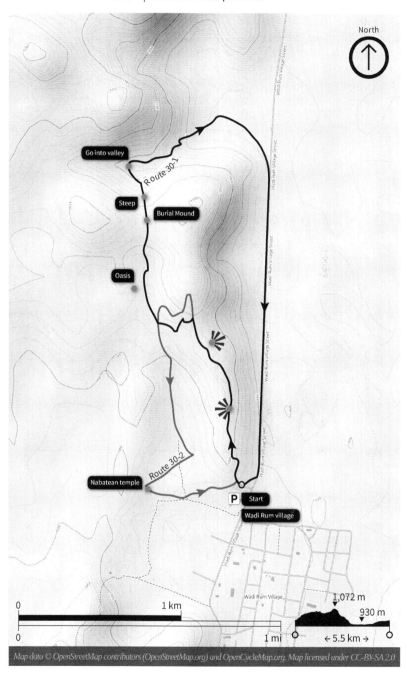

Keep the mountain to your right and continue until you arrive back at the road. Follow this to the right into Wadi Rum village.

Getting There

Please see the general notes for Wadi Rum and southern Jordan for directions to the Wadi Rum visitors' center and Wadi Rum village.

About the Nabatean Temple

- The temple was discovered in Wadi Rum by Savignac in 1932. Savignac and Horsfield undertook the first excavations in 1933 and recorded Nabatean, Greek and Thamudic inscriptions and graffiti at the temple and at Ain Shallalah (the "Real" Lawrence of Arabia Springs) *(» page 230)*.
- The Nabateans were ancient Arabs of southern Jordan, Canaan and the northern part of Arabia, whose oasis settlements gave the name of "Nabatene" to the borderland between Syria and Arabia, from the Euphrates to the Red Sea.
- In 1959, Diana Kirkbride and her team suggested that the temple was built in three phases starting in the second half of the reign of the Nabatean King Rabel II (r. 70-106AD).
- The temple was allegedly last used in the 4th century AD.
- In 1962, the Department of Antiquities began a large-scale clearing operation, exposing more than 2,800 m^2 of antiquities.
- An earthquake in 1995 caused severe damage to the temple, several villas, and building complex.
- L. Tolbecq excavated the temple site in 1999 and concluded that the Nabatean temple was first built in the reign of Aretas IV (r. 9BC-40AD) on the site of an earlier Thamudic temple.

Trail Notes

- This trail takes a couple of hours and is hard work. Don't do this if it has been raining as it can be slippery.
- This is an isolated area with no mobile phone reception. Care must be taken here.

Extended - Alternative E-trail Versions We have included two alternative routes you can hike near the Nabatean Temple in Wadi Rum. The Nabatean Temple Trail - More Rock Scrambling version requires more agility and navigation skills. The trail is for advanced hikers only who are not afraid of climbing steep rocks. In contrast, the Nabatean Temple Trail Short - To Temple version of the trail is more suitable for leisure hikers interested in a shorter, less demanding trail that involves significantly less rock scrambling and that is 1.5 hours shorter in duration.

GPS FILE	30-1 NABATEAN TEMPLE TRAIL - MORE ROCK SCRAMBLING	30-2 NABATEAN TEMPLE TRAIL SHORT - TO TEMPLE
Duration:	3.5 hours	2 hours
Level:	Advanced	Moderate
Starting Point Coordinates:	N29 34.694 E35 25.172	N29 34.694 E35 25.172
Starting Point:	Wadi Rum village.	Wadi Rum village.
Is a Four Wheel Drive Car Required?	A 4x4 car is not required. You can park a normal car in the village's parking lot.	A 4x4 car is not required. You can park a normal car in the village's parking lot.
Distance:	5.6 km (3.5 miles)	3.5 km (2.2 miles)
Highest Point:	1,089 m (3,574 ft.)	1,073 m (3,519 ft.)
Lowest Point:	923 m (3,027 ft.)	846 m (2,776 ft.)
Difference in Elevation:	166 m (547 ft.)	227 m (743 ft.)
Trail Type:	Circular Trail	Circular Trail
Is a GPS Device Required?	Yes	Yes
The Nearest Point with Amenities:	Wadi Rum village has toilets, shops and restaurants.	Wadi Rum village has toilets, shops and restaurants.

Magnificent Views from the Nabatean Temple Trail

Video Notes

0:12	-	The turn-off to Wadi Rum at the Desert Highway (Route 15).
0:21	-	The gate at the Wadi Rum visitors' center.
0:26	-	Starting point of the trail is at the parking lot in Wadi Rum village.
1:00	-	The Nabatean temple seen from the trail.
1:37	-	Expect some rock scrambling if you do not stay in the valley.
1:46	-	Views of the magnificent wadi and mountains.
2:19	-	Oasis in the wadi.

Wadi Rum and Southern Jordan

Rahma Bedouin Camel Trail

Trail

31

Undoubtedly one of the most impressive and pristine deserts in Jordan, Rahma (Rahmeh) in Wadi Araba north of Aqaba is a unique hiking area rarely visited by tourists. The area offers a range of high quality features: a Siq, exceptionally beautiful dunes, hills, rocky outcrops and even some vegetation in the middle of the desert. The views are great, and you will experience a tremendous sense of space and isolation in the vastness of this landscape. The area is truly exceptional and equals, if not surpasses, the beauty of Wadi Rum.

Introduction

The trail is in an isolated area with little or no mobile phone reception, and you are unlikely to encounter assistance if needed. Care must be taken here, as this trail cannot be followed without a GPS device loaded with our E-trail. Hiking in this part of Wadi Araba is superb, but there are virtually no marked trails.

You need a 4X4 car to start the trail in the wadi. Alternatively, you can hike from the Dead Sea Highway if you have a normal car.

Trail Description

Assuming you have a normal car, walk from the Dead Sea Highway towards the mountain range and the multi-colored cliffs near the riverbed and the sand dunes. Navigate the sand dunes on your right and go straight on to the south-east over desolate stone and sand hills onto a grey crest of conglomerate. You get a panorama of Wadi Araba from here and of the unusual purple valley to the south (right).

GPS FILE	31 RAHMA BEDOUIN CAMEL TRAIL
Duration:	4.5 hours
Level:	Advanced
Starting Point Coordinates:	N30 00.127 E35 09.989
Starting Point:	At the beginning of the trail.
Is a Four Wheel Drive Car Required?	Yes, unless you add 1.6 km or 1 mile (one way) to the trail hiking from the Dead Sea Highway.
Distance:	10.1 km (6.3 miles)
Highest Point:	427 m (1,401 ft.)
Lowest Point:	195 m (639 ft.)
Difference in Elevation:	232 m (762 ft.)
Trail Type:	Circular Trail
Is a GPS Device Required?	Yes
The Nearest Point with Amenities:	No services near the trail.

Continue on, keeping the purple valley in sight on your right but choosing the easiest path. Your path will soon intersect with a gully branching off the purple Siq. This gully has water-sculpted walls and groves of prickly acacia and hammada. It is a veritable forest compared to everything else around you. Descend into this gully named "Tree Valley", and follow it upstream going north (left) through interesting rock formations and keep climbing up over two rocky hills until you descend into the main wadi. You can follow this downstream (left) back to the car at any point. It is worth exploring this area.

Cross the wadi to explore the dead end Siq and continue north over dunes to a rocky outcrop, passing through globular rock formations on the way. The steady climb on soft sand may cause you a bit of pain, but don't worry about it, the views from up top

Magnificent Sand Dunes

really are worth the effort. It is a great place to have lunch and absorb the enormity of the view before you. There is plenty of exploring to be had in these mountains.

The return trip to the car is easy and approximately 5.8 km (3.6 miles) to the beginning of the trail if you came with a normal car and need to walk back to the Dead Sea Highway. Head south-west, keeping the main wadi to your left as you cross truly majestic dunes, perhaps the best to be seen in Jordan.

Getting There

From Amman

Drive south on the Dead Sea Highway (Route 65) for 206 km (128 miles) from the 7th Circle in Amman and pass the Beir Mathkour rest house and gas station on the right. Zero your odometer at the gas station and drive 56.5 km (35 miles) south to enter a gravel/semi-

paved road on the left after the main road curves right. Follow the track towards the mountains and sand dunes and drive as far as you can. Park the car near the wadi if you have a 4X4 car.

If you miss the turn-off on the Dead Sea Highway, continue driving to Rahma and follow the directions below.

From Aqaba
Leave Aqaba heading for the Dead Sea Highway (Route 65) and pass the Wadi Araba customs check-point on the outskirts of Aqaba. Drive north past the small town of Rahma and zero your odometer at the turn-off to Rahma. After 9.6 km (6 miles) from Rahma, turn right onto a gravel/semi-paved road just before the main road is curving left.

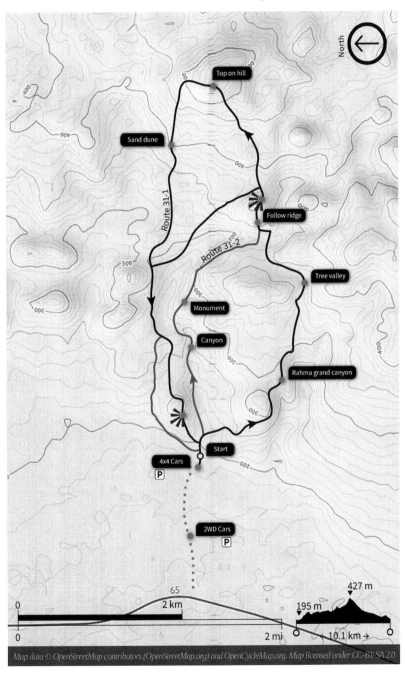

Follow the track towards the mountains and sand dune and drive as far as you can. Park the car near the wadi if you have a 4X4 car.

Trail Notes
- You most likely have to add 1.6 km (1 mile) one way to the trail hiking from the Dead Sea Highway if you come with a 2WD car.
- You can download from *www.hiking-in-jordan.com* an E-trail that leads to the starting point of the trail. The file is named "31-3 Rahma Bedouin Camel Trail Access Road."
- We recommend that you bring a local guide in case you need additional assistance during the hike.
- This is an isolated area with no mobile phone reception. Care must be taken here.

Video Notes

0:12	-	The track towards the mountains and sand dune.
0:15	-	This part of the track is not suitable for 2WD cars.
1:03	-	You will see magnificent sand dunes in the area.
1:30	-	The Siq in Rahma, although leading to a dead-end, is certainly worth a visit.
2:06	-	A fair deal of rock scrambling is involved in the trail, but you will be rewarded with magnificent views of the area. You are in unique territory.

Rahma Bedouin Camel Trail Extended

Extended - Alternative E-trail Versions

This is a longer version of the main trail that adds 2.8 km (1.7 miles) to the hike. You will be walking deeper into the desert with even greater views of the area. If you happen to have a full day and are in good shape, we recommend that you explore this trail.

Rahma Bedouin Camel Trail Through Canyon

We also have included a shorter E-trail that will lead through the canyon. This trail is less demanding, shorter in time and distance and is easier to navigate since you always have the canyon in eyesight, providing you an easy way to head back to the car.

GPS FILE	31-1 RAHMA BEDOUIN CAMEL TRAIL EXTENDED	31-2 RAHMA BEDOUIN CAMEL TRAIL THROUGH CANYON
Duration:	6 hours	4 hours
Level:	Advanced	Advanced
Starting Point Coordinates:	N30 00.127 E35 09.989	N30 00.127 E35 09.989
Starting Point:	Near the wadi at the beginning of the trail.	Near the wadi at the beginning of the trail.
Is a Four Wheel Drive Car Required?	Yes, unless you add 1.6 km or 1 mile (one way) to the trail hiking from the Dead Sea Highway.	Yes, unless you add 1.6 km or 1 mile (one way) to the trail hiking from the Dead Sea Highway.
Distance:	12.9 km (8.0 miles)	9.3 km (5.8 miles)
Highest Point:	556 m (1,825 ft.)	429 m (1,407 ft.)
Lowest Point:	195 m (639 ft.)	195 m (641 ft.)
Difference in Elevation:	361 m (1,186 ft.)	234 m (766 ft.)
Trail Type:	Circular Trail	Circular Trail
Is a GPS Device Required?	Yes	Yes
The Nearest Point with Amenities:	No services near the trail.	No services near the trail.

Wadi Rum and Southern Jordan

Seven Pillars of Wisdom

32

Introduction

The Seven Pillars of Wisdom Trail is one of our favorite hikes in Jordan. The trail is located in the vicinity of the Wadi Rum visitors' center. It is a fine walk with plenty of variety, including a dry riverbed walk through a wadi, a massive sand dune and open desert in Wadi Rum. The Seven Pillars of Wisdom is the magnificent rock formation facing the visitors' center across the wadi.

If you want to go a step further while scrambling rocks for a healthy workout, you should check out the extended versions of the trail. A GPS device is not required for the main trail.

Trail Description

From the visitors' center, walk for 1.6 km (1 mile) past the Bedouin Jeeps towards the Seven Pillars of Wisdom. As you cross the desert, take a bearing slightly to the right of the very obvious Seven Pillars massif to a sandy dry river bed.

Stay in the middle of the riverbed (do not go on the sand dunes on the right or climb the Seven Pillars on the left) and continue walking for 500 m (0.3 miles) until you reach a Y-junction. Make a left turn into a small sandy area and walk for less than 100 m (328 ft.) to the boulders and rocks. Find your way on the left through this gully and follow it up, all the time gaining altitude.

Don't forget to stop to take in the views behind you as you climb. Once you are through the rocks and the boulders, you can follow a clearly marked narrow

The Seven Pillars of Wisdom

Video Notes

0:13 - The Wadi Rum visitors' center with the Seven Pillars of Wisdom in the background.

0:21 - Walk past the Jeeps of the Bedouins near the visitors' center towards the Seven Pillars of Wisdom.

1:20 - Spectacular landscapes.

1:56 - The valley halfway along the trail.

2:35 - The valley near the sand dunes.

2:44 - Magnificent views from the top of the sand dune.

path for 0.4 km (0.2 miles) to a T-junction. Continue to the right for another 293 m (0.2 miles). At this point, the path curves to the left and walk through the canyon for another 720 m (0.45 miles).

Follow this gully up, until it narrows and you reach the gap in the Um Ishrin range.

The path goes up into the ridge straight ahead of you. The path is clearly marked and it is not too difficult to continue to the top of the rock formation.

After you have enjoyed the spectacular view over Wadi Rum, you can start your descent for a few minutes until you reach the red sand area and walk towards the left for 420 m (0.26 miles). This is the point where you will encounter a big, red sand dune.

Walk towards the top of the sand dune for a spectacular view over the valley with mountains on both sides. It takes effort, but the views from the top of the sand dune are worth it. This is also a good place to stop for a rest or lunch. If you want to stay away from the sand dunes, you can walk around them following the sand dune on your left.

Continue walking on top of the sand dunes north, hugging the mountain on your left. If you want, you can drop down to the wadi below to the right for easier walking, but don't stray off too far; keep the main mountain in sight to your left. You will pass through magnificent mountains here.

After walking north on the sand dunes for 1.9 km (1.2 miles), turn left at the end of the valley and walk for 1.4 km (0.9 miles) with the Seven Pillars of Wisdom rock formation on your left. At this point, the visitors' center will come into view again. Continue across the desert for another 1.3 km (0.8 miles) to arrive at the Wadi Rum visitors' center.

GPS FILE	32 SEVEN PILLARS OF WISDOM
Duration:	4 hours
Level:	Moderate
Starting Point Coordinates:	N29 38.385 E35 26.051
Starting Point:	Wadi Rum visitors' center.
Is a Four Wheel Drive Car Required?	A 4x4 car is not required. You can park a normal car at the visitors' center.
Distance:	10.1 km (6.3 miles)
Highest Point:	1,017 m (3,337 ft.)
Lowest Point:	833 m (2,733 ft.)
Difference in Elevation:	184 m (604 ft.)
Trail Type:	Circular Trail
Is a GPS Device Required?	No
The Nearest Point with Amenities:	The visitors' center has toilets, shops and a restaurant.

About the Seven Pillars of Wisdom

- "The Seven Pillars of Wisdom: A Triumph" is an autobiographical work of T. E. Lawrence ("Lawrence of Arabia") who served as a British liaison officer with rebel forces during the Arab Revolt against the Ottoman Turks from 1916 to 1918. The forebears of the Bedouins here, part of the Howeitat tribe, were fierce warriors in the Arab Revolt.
- While locals claim T.E. Lawrence either named the formation, or named his book after it, neither is true. Lawrence took the title of his book from the Old Testament's Book of Proverbs, 9:1: "Wisdom hath builded her house, she hath hewn out her seven pillars" (King James version).
- The original name for this rock formation is Jebel al Mazmar, and it was renamed by locals in the 1980s as the Seven Pillars of Wisdom to capitalize on Western fascination with Lawrence's exploits.
- For your edification, the Seven Pillars of Wisdom referred to are prudence, knowledge, discretion,

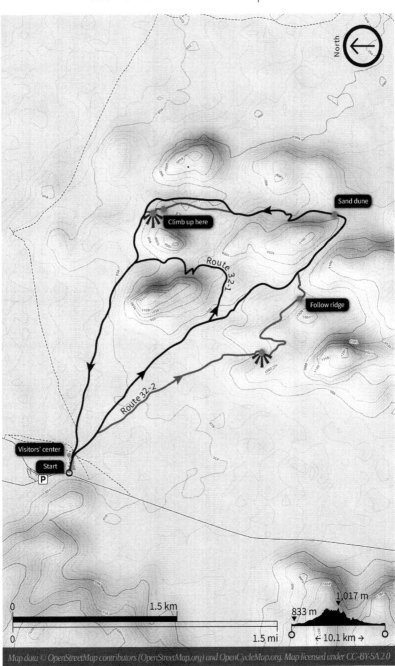

counsel, sound judgment, understanding and power. Keep working on them.

Geology
- The Seven Pillars of Wisdom are part of the mountain range of Jebel um Ishrin. This range consists of hard red Cambium sandstone overlying very hard, dark-hued Precambrian basement. There is some creamy-white sandstone on top.
- These softer sandstones tend to erode into domes, and are more prevalent in the south and east of the Wadi Rum Reserve. You see them on this walk when you get to the other side of the Ishrin range. You can see a clear demarcation between the darker basement stone underneath, the red and then white sandstone on top. This is also apparent in the Jebel Rum range to the west.

Getting There
Please see the general notes for Wadi Rum and southern Jordan for directions to the Wadi Rum visitors' center.

Trail Notes
The standard walk is mostly an easy walk along a dry riverbed with occasional clambering to get over large boulders and quite a big dune which takes effort to navigate.

Extended - Alternative E-trail Versions
The alternative - extended E-trail versions of the trail add rock scrambling in interesting but more demanding terrain.

Although it is shorter, the *Seven Pillars of Wisdom - Rock Scrambling* variant is also more demanding than the much easier main trail. It involves scrambling on rocks, but provides greater views through fairly difficult terrain. On this trail, you will not see the sand dunes.

The *Seven Pillars of Wisdom Extended:* If you want to extend the standard trail with more views and additional rock scrambling, than this E-trail may be of interest to you. It extends the hike, throws in interesting terrain, extra views to the west and requires more effort.

GPS FILE	32-1 SEVEN PILLARS OF WISDOM ROCK SCRAMBLING	32-2 SEVEN PILLARS OF WISDOM EXTENDED
Duration:	3.5 hours	4.5 hours
Level:	Advanced	Advanced
Starting Point Coordinates:	N29 38.385 E35 26.051	N29 38.385 E35 26.051
Starting Point:	Wadi Rum visitors' center.	Wadi Rum visitors' center.
Is a Four Wheel Drive Car Required?	A 4x4 car is not required. You can park a normal car at the visitors' center.	A 4x4 car is not required. You can park a normal car at the visitors' center.
Distance:	6.6 km (4.1 miles)	10.3 km (6.4 miles)
Highest Point:	1,018 m (3,340 ft.)	1,028 m (3,374 ft.)
Lowest Point:	830 m (2,724 ft.)	830 m (2,724 ft.)
Difference in Elevation:	188 m (616 ft.)	198 m (650 ft.)
Trail Type:	Circular Trail	Circular Trail
Is a GPS Device Required?	Yes	Yes
The Nearest Point with Amenities:	The visitors' center has toilets, shops and a restaurant.	The visitors' center has toilets, shops and a restaurant.

The Wadi Rum Visitors' Center Seen from a Distance

Legal Notice

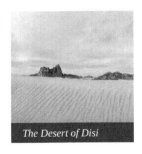

The Desert of Disi

Please read the following terms and conditions carefully as they govern your use of the Hiking in Jordan Guide. Your use of the Hiking in Jordan Guide constitutes your acceptance without modification of all of the terms, conditions, and notices contained herein.

Acceptance of Terms through Use

In consideration of your agreement to these Terms of Use and for other valuable consideration, we grant to you a limited, non-exclusive, revocable and non-transferable license to access and use the Hiking in Jordan Guide. We reserve all rights not expressly granted in this Agreement. We reserve the right to make modifications, improvements, deletions, or amendments to the Hiking in Jordan Guide at any time we deem appropriate. Any and all relevant portions of this Agreement will apply automatically to all modifications, improvements, deletions, and/or amendments as they appear.

Disclaimer

Please read the following disclaimer before hiking in Jordan and using the Hiking in Jordan Guide. Contents of the Hiking in Jordan Guide, defined and referred to as the hard copy and e-Book of the Hiking in Jordan Guide, associated websites, blogs, apps and any other means of communication are intended for educational purposes only and should not be relied upon for any practical, medical, legal or financial decisions.

Any opinions expressed in the Hiking in Jordan Guide are the opinions of the authors and not necessarily of the authors' affiliates, family, and former and current employers. The authors, their affiliates, family and former and current employers make NO representations or warranties about the suitability, reliability, timeliness, appropriateness, or accuracy of the information in the Hiking in Jordan Guide and;

- Will NOT be liable for damages of any kind arising from the use of the Hiking in Jordan Guide, including, but not limited to, direct, incidental, punitive, and consequential damages;
- Do NOT accept any liability or responsibility for any accident or injury inside the reserves and other hiking areas described in the Hiking in Jordan Guide and/or those caused by the usage of the trails and GPS E-trails described in the Hiking in Jordan Guide;
- Do NOT assume any responsibility or liability for the accuracy of hike directions and trail conditions in the Hiking in Jordan Guide. Although every effort has been made by the authors to ensure that the Hiking in Jordan Guide provides accurate information on trails in Jordan, the condition of trails may change over time;
- Do NOT accept liability for your personal safety on any of the trails and hiking areas described in the Hiking in Jordan Guide. The information in the Hiking in Jordan Guide is a resource only. It is your responsibility to be properly prepared for a hike and you alone are responsible for your own safety.

Hiking is a Personal Choice Hiking and using trail descriptions and maps in the Hiking in Jordan Guide and using GPS equipment is a personal choice and requires that YOU understand that you are personally responsible for any actions you may take based on the information in the Hiking in Jordan Guide. Using any information in the Hiking in Jordan Guide is your own personal responsibility.

Hiking and associated trail activities can be dangerous and with all outdoor activities can result in injury and/or death. Hiking exposes you to risks especially in developing countries. While hiking in Jordan, you may encounter a number of risks you should be aware of. These relate to risks associated with hiking, climbing or bouldering in Jordan, including but not limited to:

- Weather conditions such as flash floods, wind, rain, snow and lightning;
- Hazardous plants or wild animals;
- Objects hidden under water or in sand such as discarded construction materials and fence wiring;
- Your own physical condition, or your own acts or omissions;
- Conditions of roads, trails, or terrain, and accidents connected with their use and receiving First Aid, emergency treatment or other medical services you may receive and/or require;
- Accidents and injuries occurring while traveling to or from the hiking areas;
- The inaccessibility or remoteness of the hiking areas which may delay rescue and medical treatment;
- The distance of the hiking areas from emergency medical facilities and law enforcement personnel.

Limitation of Liability

LIMITATION OF LIABILITY: TO THE FULLEST EXTENT PERMISSIBLE PURSUANT TO APPLICABLE LAW, NEITHER GREGORY MAASSEN, CHRIS GRANT, THEIR AFFILIATES, FAMILIES AND FORMER AND CURRENT EMPLOYERS NOR ANY OTHER PARTY INVOLVED IN CREATING, PRODUCING OR DELIVERING THE HIKING IN JORDAN GUIDE IS LIABLE FOR ANY DIRECT, INCIDENTAL, CONSEQUENTIAL, INDIRECT, EXEMPLARY, OR PUNITIVE DAMAGES ARISING OUT OF A USER'S ACCESS TO, OR USE OF THE HIKING IN JORDAN GUIDE.

You assume all risk of errors and/or omissions in the Hiking in Jordan Guide including the transmission or translation of information.

In addition, you acknowledge, understand, and agree that there are risks, including but not limited to, the risk of physical harm, the risk of dealing with strangers, foreign nationals, underage persons, or people acting under false pretenses.

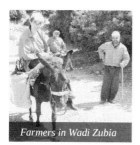
Farmers in Wadi Zubia

You assume all risks associated with dealing with the vendors with whom you may come in contact with through the Hiking in Jordan Guide.

You assume full responsibility for implementing sufficient procedures and updates to satisfy your requirements for the accuracy and suitability of the Hiking in Jordan Guide including the information provided therein.

By using this guide, you agree that any action brought by you will be brought within the Hashemite Kingdom of Jordan and that you agree to adhere to the exclusive jurisdiction of the Jordanian courts. You further agree that the laws in force in the said Hashemite Kingdom of Jordan shall govern this agreement.

Please acknowledge sponsors, copyright holders and authors if you use their work. You cannot sell any of the materials in this Hiking Guide or use them for any other commercial purpose unless otherwise indicated.

Copyrights All materials in this Hiking Guide have been included with the permission of copyright holders and/or when allowed under legislation. Please note that we retain full copyright of the text in this Hiking Guide, the cover design and GPS files. The hiking videos and photos are licensed under the CC BY-SA license. The relevant licenses are displayed in this Hiking Guide. Any of the above conditions can be waived if you obtain permission from the copyright holder.

As with the contents of this Hiking Guide, the E-trails are protected by copyright laws. Please refrain from posting the GPS files on the Internet. This allows us to maintain high quality standards while owners of this Hiking Guide benefit from the E-trails and other great resources that come with the Hiking Guide.

Piracy

We take the protection of our copyright and licenses very seriously. If you come across any illegal copies of the Hiking Guide, in any form, on the Internet, in Jordan or elsewhere, please provide us with the location address or website name so that we can pursue a remedy. We appreciate your help in protecting our ability to bring you valuable content combined with the additional resources available through the website.

Appendix

Directions

Arabic Phrase

The following translations have been provided by Jacky Bedrossian, author of "Say it in Arabic, Basic Arabic for Jordan."

You can buy her excellent book in bookstores in Amman and Aqaba. Jacky can be reached at: *Bedrossian.62@gmail.com*.

	THE ARABIC AS IT IS PRONOUNCED IN ENGLISH	AS IT IS WRITTEN IN ARABIC
About Nature		
I like nature.	Ba-h'ib il ta-bee-a' Bah'ib il tabeea'	بحب الطبيعة
I like to walk in nature.	Ba-h'ib am-shee bil ta-bee-a' Bah'ib amshee bil tabeea'	بحب امشي بالطبيعة
Jordan is a beautiful country.	Il oo-r-doon ba-lad h'iloo Il Urdoon balad h'iloo	الاردن بلد حلو
I am in Jordan on holiday.	Ana ib ot-la bil Ur-doon Ana be-otla bil Urdoon	انا بعطلة بالاردن

	THE ARABIC AS IT IS PRONOUNCED IN ENGLISH	AS IT IS WRITTEN IN ARABIC
This is a beautiful wadi.	Ha-tha (th as the) il wa-dee ki-teer hi-loo Hatha il wadi kiteer hiloo	هذا الوادي كتير حلو
This is a beautiful area.	Ha-thee (th as the) il man-ta-ka ki-teer hil-wa Hathi il mantaka kiteer Hilwa	هاذي المنطقة كتير حلوة
This is a great waterfall.	Ha-tha (th as the) sha-lal ki-teer h'i-loo, bee-ja-nin Hatha shalal kiteer h'iloo, beejanin	هذا شلال كتير حلو، بيجنن
The desert is beautiful.	Il sah'-raa' ki-teer hil-wa Ilsah'raa' kiteer hilwa	الصحراء كتير حلوة
We are walking for a few hours.	Rah' nit-ma-sha a-kam min sa-a' Rah' nitmasha akam min saa'	راح نتمشى اكم من ساعة
Directions		
Can you show me the direction to the Dead Sea Highway?	Tig-dar it-dil-nee la-te-reeg il ba'h'ar il may-it? Tigdar itdilni la tereeg il bah'ar il mayit?	تقدر اتدلني لطريق البحر الميت؟
Where is the Dead Sea Highway?	Wayne te-rreeg il ba-h'ar il may-it? Wayne terreeg il bah'ar il mayit?	وين طريق البحر الميت ؟
Can you show me the direction to the Kings Highway?	Tig-dar it-dil-nee a'l tareeg Il mil-oo-kee? Tigdar itdilni a'l tareeg il milooki	تقدر اتدلني عالطريق الملوكي؟

	The Arabic as it is pronounced in English	As it is written in Arabic
Where is the Kings Highway?	Wen il ta-reeg il mil-oo-kee? Wen il tareeg il milooki?	وين الطريق الملوكي؟
Can you show me the direction to the Desert Road?	Tig-dar it-dil-nee a'l-ta-reeg il-sah'-ra-wee? Tigdar itdilni a'l tareeg il sah'rawi?	تقدر اتدلني عالطريق الصحراوي؟
Where is the Desert Road?	Wen il tareeg il sah'rawee?	وين الطريق الصحراوي؟
Can you show me the direction to Aqaba?	Tig-dar it-dil-nee a'la ta-reeg il A-qa-ba? Tigdar itdilnee a'la tareeg il Aqaba?	تقدر اتدلني على طريق العقبة؟
Where is the Aqaba Road?	Wen tareeg il Aqaba?	وين طريق العقبة؟
Can you show me the direction to Amman?	Tig-dar it-dil-nee a'-la ta-reeg A'-mman? Tigdar itdilni a'la tareeg A'mman?	تقدر اتدلني على طريق عمان؟
Where is the Amman Road?	Wen tareeg A'mman?	وين طريق عمان؟
Can you show me the direction to Madaba?	Tig-dar it-dil-nee a'-la. ta-reeg Madaba? Tigdar itdilni a'la tareeg Madaba?	تقدر اتدلني على طريق مأدبا؟
Where is the Madaba Road?	Wen tareeg Madaba?	وين طريق مأدبا؟
Can you show me the direction to Feynan?	Tig-dar it-dil-nee a'-la ta-reeg Fee-nan? Tigdar itdilni a'la tareeg Feenan?	تقدر اتدلني على طريق فينان؟
Where is the Feynan Road?	Wen tareeg Feenan?	وين طريق فينان؟

	THE ARABIC AS IT IS PRONOUNCED IN ENGLISH	AS IT IS WRITTEN IN ARABIC
General		
Good morning	Sabah' el khair	صباح الخير
Reply	Sabah' el noor	صباح النور
Good afternoon *or* Good evening	Masa el khair	مساء الخير
Reply	Masa el noor	مساء النور
Hello	Marh'aba	مرحبا
Reply to hello	Mar-h'a-ba	مرحبا
Greeting	As salamu a'laikom	السلام علكيم
Reply	Waa'alaikum as salam	وعليكم السلام
Another way of greeting any time of the day. *or* Extremely polite way of thanking someone.	Ya'tiki el a'afya (f) Ya'tik el a'afya (m) Yatiku el a'afya (pl)	يعطيكي العافية يعطيك العافية يعطيكو العافية
Reply	Allah ya'fiki (f) Allah yafik (m) Allah ya'fiku (pl)	الله يبعافيكي الله يبعافيك الله يبعافييكو
What is your name? (m)	Esh ismak?	ايش اسمَك؟
What is your name? (f)	Esh ismik?	ايش اسمِك؟
Do you speak English?	Ib-teh'-kee in-glee-zee? Ibteh'ki inglizi?	ابتحكي انجليزي؟

	THE ARABIC AS IT IS PRONOUNCED IN ENGLISH	AS IT IS WRITTEN IN ARABIC
I do not speak Arabic.	Ana ma bah'-kee ara-bee Ana ma bah'ki arabi	انا ما بحكي عربي
I do not understand Arabic.	Ana ma bafham arabi	انا ما بفهم عربي
What?	Esh or Shu?	ايش / شو ؟
Why?	Lesh?	ليش ؟
Pardon	A'fwan	عفواً؟
Where?	Wayne?	وين؟
When?	Emta?	امتة ؟
Who?	Meen?	مين ؟
How?	Keef?	كييف ؟
Yes	Naa'm	نعم
No	La	لا
Thank you	Shukran	شكراً
Do you want to drink tea? (M)	Tishrab chai?	تشرب شاي ؟
Do you want to drink tea? (F)	Tishrabi chai?	تشربي شاي ؟
Do you want to drink tea? (Pl)	Tishraboo chai?	تشربو شاي؟
Where can I buy water?	Wayne bagdar ashtri my?	وين بقدر اشتري مي ؟ (ماء)
Where is the shop that sells water?	Wayne fee mah'al bee-bea' (ea as earth) my?	وين في محل ببيع مي ؟ (ماء)

Travel Notes

Dear Sir/Madam,

We are on holiday in Jordan. We parked our car because we are walking for a few hours in this beautiful area. We should be back before sunset.

In case you need to reach us, our telephone number is:

Thank you so much!

عزيزي سيدي / سيدتي
احنا بعطلة بالاردن،صفينا سيارتنا عشان بدنا نمشي اكم من ساعة في هالمكان الحلو، راح نرجع قبل المغرب.
في حالة بدك تحكي معنا؟
رقم الموبايل:
شكرا كتير

Dear Sir/Madam,

We are on holiday in Jordan. We parked our car because we are walking for a day in this beautiful area. We should be back tomorrow.

In case you need to reach us, our telephone number is:

Thank you so much!

عزيزي سيدي / سيدتي
احنا بعطلة بالاردن، صفينا سيارتنا عشان بدنا نمشي ليوم كامل في هالمكان الحلو، المفروض نرجع بكري,
في حالة بدك تحكي معنا؟
رقم الموبايل :
شكر كتير

Dear Sir/Madam,

We are on holiday in Jordan and we are walking for a day in this beautiful area. The area we are in is described in this book. According to the book, it is permissible to walk here.

Thank you so much!

عزيزي سيدي / سيدتي
احنا بعطلة بالاردن، صفينا سيارتنا عشان بدنا نمشي ليوم كامل في هالمكان الحلو،
المكان الي احنا في وصفو موجود في هذا الكتاب,
وبحسب الكتاب مسموح نمشي في هالمكان.
في حالة بدك تحكي معنا
رقم الموبايل :
شكر كتير

Dear Sir/Madam,

Thank you so much for your offer to assist us. We really appreciate it if you can guide us to the nearest police station.

Thank you so much!

عزيزي سيدي/ سيدتي
شكراً كثير على المساعدة، عن جد احنا مقدرينلك هذا الأشي , اذا في مجال اتوصلنا لعند اقرب مركز شرطة

شكراً كثير

Dear Sir/Madam,

Thank you so much for your offer to assist us. We are lost and do not know where we left the car. Have you seen our car? We really appreciate it if you can show us where you saw the car.

Thank you so much!

عزيزي سيدي / سيدتي :
شكراً كثير على المساعدة عن جد احنا مقدرينلك هذا الأشي.
احنا ضعنا ومش عارفين وين تركنا سيارتنا, شفت سيارتنا؟ بتعمل معروف لو اتوصلنا على محل ما شفت السيارة.
شكراً كثير

Dear Sir/Madam,

Thank you so much for your offer to assist us. We need to see a doctor. Can you help us?

Thank you so much!

عزيزي سيدي / سيدتي :
شكراً كثير على المساعدة عن جد احنا مقدرينلك هذا الأشي.
بدنا انروح عالدكتور, تقدر اتساعدنا؟
شكراً كثير

Dear Sir/Madam,

Thank you so much for your offer to assist us. Our cell phone is not working. Can we use your phone to call this number: ?

Thank you so much!

عزيزي سيدي / سيدتي :
شكراً كثير على المساعدة عن جد احنا مقدرينلك هذا الأشي.
التلفون (الموبايل) تبعنا مش شغال, اذا في مجال نحكي من تلفونك (موبايلك) على هالرقم :
شكراً كثير

Overview of GPS Files	You can download at *www.hiking-in-jordan.com* the following GPS E-trails.		
GPS FILE NUMBER	TRAIL NAME	PAGE	WAYPOINT CODE
01	Ajloun Castle Circuit	»28	ACC
02-1	Ajloun Castle Trail - Route 1	»33	ACT
02-2	Ajloun Castle Trail - Route 2		
	References: • Jordan Tourism Board www.visitjordan.com/default.aspx?tabid=169 • www.jordanbeauty.com/AjlunCastle.html • www.en.wikipedia.org/wiki/Ajlun_Castle • www.gomagjordan.com/ajloun-castle • www.rscn.org.jo		
03	Pella Mountain Trail	»37	PM
03-1	Pella Mountain Ridge Trail		
03-2	Pella Mountain Trail - Car Drop Off		
	References: • Near Eastern Archaeology Foundation - The Pella Excavation Project of the University of Sydney: http://sydney.edu.au/arts/sophi/neaf/excavations/index.shtml. • Pella in Jordan, a Brief History of the Site, by Ben Churcher-Astarte Resources 2008-www.astarte.com.au with reference to the Pella Project, University of Sydney. • Charles Leonard Irby and James Mangles (1823) - Travels in Egypt and Nubia, Syria, and the Holy Land: Including a Journey Round the Dead Sea, and Through the Country East of the Jordan.		
04	Wadi Zubia Forest Walk	»44	WZ
04-1	Driving Directions from Ajloun Castle to Wadi Zubia		

GPS FILE NUMBER	TRAIL NAME	PAGE	WAYPOINT CODE
	References: • Dr. Saeed Damhoureyeh-Ecology, Trip report Shaumari reserve, Azraq reserve, Qasr Harranah and Qusayr Amra • Jordanian Tourism Board, Eco Jordan Map-www.visitjordan.com/e_book/EcoJordan Map • www.visitjordan.com • www.rscn.org.jo		
05	Dana Feynan Trail	»52	DF
	References: • RSCN: www.rscn.org.jo • The Jordanian Tourism Board: http://visitjordan.com • UNESCO: http://whc.unesco.org • G. Barker, D. Gilbertson and D. Mattingly (eds.) 2007. Archaeology and Desertification: The Wadi Faynan Landscape Survey, Southern Jordan		
06	Little Petra Trail	»59	LP
	References: • The Department of Cross-Cultural and Regional Studies at the University of Copenhagen hosts a database of the documents, slides etc. from the Diana Kirkbride Archive available at http://tors.kb.dk/dvn/dv/Kirkbride • Kirkbride, D.V.W. (1968) Beidha: Early Neolithic village life south of the Dead Sea. in: Antiquity, Volume 42 263-274 • Douglas C. Corner-ERSI (April 2003): Environmental History at an Early Prehistoric Village: An Application of Cultural Site Analysis at Beidha, in Southern Jordan, Journal of GIS in Archaeology, Volume I		

GPS File Number	Trail Name	Page	Waypoint Code
07	Mukawir Mini Circuit	»69	MM
	References: • Vörös, Győző. "Machaerus: Where Salome Danced and John the Baptist Was Beheaded." Biblical Archaeology Review, Sep/Oct 2012, 30–41, 68 • www.biblicalarchaeology.org/daily/bibli-cal-sites-places/biblical-archaeology-sites/machaerus-beyond-the-beheading-of-john-the-baptist/ • www.visitjordan.com/default.aspx?tabid=74 • www.kinghussein.gov.jo/tourism6b.html • www.romanaqueducts.info/aquasite/machaerus/ • G. Garbrecht and Y. Peleg: The Water Supply of the Desert Fortresses in the Jordan Valley (in: The Biblical Archaeologist vol 57-3 (1994) pag 161 ff)		
08	High Place of Sacrifice Trail	»76	PHT
08-1	High Place of Sacrifice Trail to Little Petra Route 1	»86	
08-2	High Place of Sacrifice Trail to Little Petra Route 2		
09	Petra Monastery Trail	»90	PMT
09-1	Petra Monastery Trail to Little Petra	»96	
	References: • http://en.wikipedia.org/wiki/Petra • www.visitjordan.com/default.aspx?tabid=63 • www.visitpetra.jo		
10	Rummana Mountain Trail	»100	RMT
10-1	Rummana Mountain Trail Walking from Visitors Center and Cave Trail		
	Reference: • The Royal Society for the Conservation of Nature (RSCN)		
11	Wadi Bin Hammad Tropical Rain Forest Trail	»105	WB

GPS File Number	Trail Name	Page	Waypoint Code
11-1	Wadi Bin Hammad Tropical Rain Forest Trail - Directions		
12	Wadi Ghuweir Trail to Feynan	»112	WG
	References: • RSCN: www.rscn.org.jo • The Jordanian Tourism Board: http://visitjordan.com • G. Barker, D. Gilbertson and D. Mattingly (eds.) 2007. Archaeology and Desertification: The Wadi Faynan Landscape Survey, Southern Jordan		
13	Wadi Al Karak Waterfalls	»125	WK
13-1	Wadi Al Karak Access Road		
14	Wadi Assal Trail	»132	WA
14-1	Wadi Assal Access Road		
15	Wadi Attun Hot Springs Trail	»138	WAH
16	Wadi Himara Palm Trees and Waterfall Trail	»143	WHPT
16-1	Wadi Himara Palm Trees and Waterfall Trail with Detour		
17	Wadi Himara Panorama Trail	»149	WHP
18	Wadi Mujib Malaqi Trail	»155	WMM
	References: • RSCN Mujib Biosphere Reserve • UNESCO: http://whc.unesco.org/en/tentativelists/5158/		
19	Wadi Mujib Siq Trail	»162	WMS
20	Wadi Mukheiris Formation Trail	»166	WM
	References: • Schoch, R.R. (2011). "A trematosauroid temnospondyl from the Middle Triassic of Jordan." The Fossil Record 14 (2): 119–127 • www.ucmp.berkeley.edu/vertebrates/tetrapods/tetrafr.html		

GPS File Number	Trail Name	Page	Waypoint Code
	• Issa M. Makhlouf, Fluvial/tidal interaction at the southern Tethyan strandline during Triassic Mukheiris times in central Jordan • Geological Model and Groundwater Aspects of the Area Surrounding Eastern Shores of Dead Sea (DS)–Jordan Akawwi, E Kakish, M, Hadadin, N • Bandel, K., Khoury, H., 1981. Lithostratigraphy of the Triassic in Jordan. Erlangen. Facies 4, 1 – 26		
21	Wadi Numeira Siq Trail	» 172	WN
21-1	Wadi Numeira Siq Trail Access Road Only		
22	Wadi Weida Trail Only	» 178	WW
22-1	Wadi Weida Access Road From Dead Sea		
23	Abu Burqa Dam Lookout	» 188	AB
	References: • Building Sustainable Livelihoods-Jordan Human Development Report, MoPIC/ UNDP, 2004 • www.ccjo.com/Projects/WaterWastewaterDams/ ABUBURQADAMJORDAN/tabid/248/Default. aspx • blog.jordanriver.jo/the-story-of-abu-wael-2/ • www.birdforum.net/showthread. php?t=220175&page=2		
24	Adami Trail - Jordan's Tallest Mountain	» 194	AT
24-1	Adami 4x4 Drive and Trail		
25-1	Bedouin Camp Circuit Route 1	» 200	BC
25-2	Bedouin Camp Circuit Route 2		
26-1	Burial Mound and Oryx Trail	» 207	BM
26-3	Burial Mound and Oryx Trail - Extended to Ibex Lookout		
27	French Fortress Trail	» 214	FF
27-1	French Fortress Trail with Access Road Track		
28	Ibex Canyon Lookout	» 222	IC
28-1	Ibex Canyon Lookout Rock Scrambling Route I		

GPS FILE NUMBER	TRAIL NAME	PAGE	WAYPOINT CODE
28-2	Ibex Canyon Lookout Rock Scrambling Route II		
29	Lawrence of Arabia Spring	»230	LA
	References: • Isabelle Ruben and Ghassan Nasser. Review of the Archaeology of the Wadi Rum Protected Area, July 1999 • T.E. Lawrence, The Seven Pillars of Wisdom		
30	Nabatean Temple Trail	»236	NT
30-1	Nabatean Temple Trail - More Rock Scrambling		
30-2	Nabatean Temple Trail Short - To Temple		
	References: • Isabelle Ruben and Ghassan Nasser. Review of the Archaeology of the Wadi Rum Protected Area, July 1999 • http://qedar.org/nabataeans.html		
31	Rahma Bedouin Camel Trail	»244	RB
31-1	Rahma Bedouin Camel Trail Extended		
31-2	Rahma Bedouin Camel Trail Through Canyon		
31-3	Rahma Bedouin Camel Trail Access Road		
32	Seven Pillars of Wisdom	»251	SP
32-1	Seven Pillars of Wisdom Rock Scrambling		
32-2	Seven Pillars of Wisdom Trail Extended		
	References: • UNESCO: http://whc.unesco.org/en/list/1377		

About the Authors

Chris Grant

Gregory Maassen

Chris Grant, Bsc (Hons)/LLB, is a biologist and was for two years senior advisor in the Wadi Rum Reserve in Jordan. He has traveled extensively hiking and wildlife spotting. He currently lives in Australia and works in environmental conservation.

Gregory Maassen, Ph.D., is a development professional who has implemented long-term technical assistance programs throughout the world. He was based in Aqaba for three years where he frequently organized hiking trips to Petra, Wadi Rum and Rahma.

14166979R00157

Made in the USA
San Bernardino, CA
18 August 2014